*The
Connell Guide
to*

Louis XIV

by William Doyle

Contents

Introduction   4

THE FIRST REIGN, 1643-1660s:
a turbulent apprenticeship

How was France governed during the king's minority?   5
What steps did Mazarin take to raise money?   8
Did Mazarin overplay his hand?   12
What caused the first Fronde, and how did it end?   15
How were the rebels finally defeated?   19
What steps did Mazarin take to prepare the monarch for power?   22
How have historians judged the king's first reign?   29

THE SECOND REIGN, 1660s-1680s:
power and glory

How did the king establish his personal authority?   33
Whom did he rely on to help him?   36
How did the king impose his authority on France?   40
How successful were the king's attempts to achieve domination abroad?   50
What did he achieve in his second reign?   57

THE THIRD REIGN, 1680s-1715:
the limits of ambition

Why did things go wrong?   62
How did French expansion lose momentum?   69

How expensive were these military adventures?	75
Why another war?	76
Why did the king back down?	82
How have historians judged the third reign?	85

Legacies, 1715-1815

In what state did Louis XIV leave his kingdom?	88
What was Louis XIV's cultural legacy?	95
What was the final result of the Sun King's ambition?	101

NOTES

Richelieu	*8*
Venal office	*10*
Lit de justice	*14*
Titles and mottoes	*30*
Duels	*39*
Absolutism	*40*
Louis XIV in his own words	*42*
Cultural glory	*46*
Royal residences	*48*
Ten Facts about Louis XIV	*60*
Gallicanism	*65*
A short chronology	*109*
Bibliography	*111*

Introduction

When he was baptised in 1643, five years after he was born, the son of Louis XIII of France and his Spanish queen, Anne of Austria, was given two names: Louis, and God-given (*Dieudonné*). By then, he also had a younger brother; but his birth to a 37-year-old mother, childless since marriage in 1615 and seldom in her husband's company, still seemed like a miracle.

The queen certainly thought so. In gratitude she vowed to build a vast commemorative church, to be served by Benedictine nuns: the Val-de-Grâce. In 1645 the God-given child himself, now King Louis XIV, laid the foundation stone. Governing the kingdom in her son's name, the regent-queen was able to spend what she liked to build it on a lavish scale. When she died in 1666 it was almost finished, and by then her son was a mature monarch. The completion the next year of this monastic church – built as a thank you to God for his existence – crowned the transition from the turbulent "first reign" of his youth and early manhood, to a second reign in which he exuded serene confidence and proud triumph. Both phases lasted around a generation. So did a final third reign, triumphant, too, in its way, but also marked by years of misery and humiliation.

The legacy of Louis XIV's 72 years on the throne was complex and long-lasting. The memory haunted the three further generations that separated his death in 1715 from the Revolution which sought to expunge it for good. The revolutionaries pulled down his statues, destroyed the monarchy and the court which he had created, and condemned the social structures underpinning them. Yet, just like him, they sought to overawe Europe with French power; he was the only former ruler of France whom Napoleon admired. Like Napoleon, Louis XIV has always divided historical opinion. The following pages seek to explore how and why.

THE FIRST REIGN, 1643-1660s: a turbulent apprenticeship

How was France governed during the king's minority?

Until 1651, when Louis XIV reached 13, the legal age of majority, his kingdom was formally governed by his mother as queen regent. In practice, Anne of Austria's authority lasted until the death in 1661 of her inseparable partner in power, Cardinal Jules Mazarin.

Mazarin was Italian, brought into French service by Cardinal Richelieu, Louis XIII's principal minister. Though never a priest, he was made a cardinal at Richelieu's insistence in 1642. He joined Louis XIII's council, and was chosen as godfather to the heir to the throne. The queen liked him, and when she became regent one of her earliest acts was to make him her principal minister – a natural successor to Richelieu. Over the years they became so close that it was rumoured they were secretly married.

The fact that neither was French, and that she was the sister of France's main enemy, Philip IV of Spain, was strongly held against them by the great nobles who expected to share power during a royal minority. Indeed, within weeks of Mazarin's appointment some of these nobles were plotting his assassination. This conspiracy of the *Importants* was thwarted, but thereafter the regent and Mazarin took pains to conciliate and flatter the vanity of the magnates, particularly princes of the blood royal. The most significant of these were Louis XIII's feckless brother, Gaston d'Orléans, and his cousin, the Prince de Condé, whose hopes of the throne had been blighted by the belated birth of the queen's two sons.

War against the Spanish and Austrian Habsburgs, which had been raging since 1635, also served to distract the nobles' energies. Between 1643 and 1648 Condé's son Enghien (who would inherit his father's title in 1646) won a series of spectacular victories over the hitherto formidable armies of Spain.

Yet glory-hunting noblemen were probably the

Rubens's portrait of Louis XIV's mother, Anne of Austria (c. 1622)

only significant group in favour of prolonging the war. Everybody else hoped and expected that the deaths of Richelieu and Louis XIII would bring peace, and an end to the relentless pressure of new taxation that had been endured since fighting began. Tax revenues were years in arrears over much of the kingdom, and now there were destabilising rumours that unpaid demands would be written off. Massive regional tax revolts had also marked recent years, and there was a new one in the south just as the regency began.

But the war went on, and French financial difficulties only encouraged Spain, despite its own problems, to keep up the pressure. Negotiations for a general peace began in Germany in 1643, but they took an agonising five years to reach a conclusion. France's conflict with Spain remained unresolved for another 11.

What steps did Mazarin take to raise money?

Mazarin entrusted financing the war to a fellow (though naturalised) Italian, Particelli d'Emery. Particelli concluded that normal tax revenues, even if they came in punctually, could not cover wartime expenses. He therefore redoubled the use of

RICHELIEU

The ghost of Cardinal Richelieu haunted the entire reign of Louis XIV. The cardinal, principal minister of Louis XIII between 1624 and his death in 1642, was an all-powerful subject who made his royal master look like a puppet. Louis XIV was determined to avoid anything like this happening again.

Yet the cardinal taught those who succeeded him at the helm of the state that its interests were paramount and long-term, and overrode everything else — a principle known as *raison d'Etat*. He also taught them that the mainspring of French foreign policy should be opposition to the Habsburgs, and a constant search for opportunities to deprive them of territories and influence.

so-called "extraordinary" measures, pioneered under Richelieu. The range of these was enormous: they included anticipating future income, auctioning tax collection to the highest bidder, manipulating interest rates on the state's debts, and delaying payments. Meanwhile, tax exemptions and other privileges were routinely cancelled, or threatened with cancellation unless they were repurchased. Forgotten laws were reactivated so as to impose more fines, and various forms of forced loan were imposed. Many new venal offices were created, existing ones duplicated, remuneration withheld. It was government by blackmail.

Most of these schemes were devised by private financiers, who offered the crown ready money for the right to run them – at a profit. They were known as *traitants*. They raised their initial capital by

---

Organising the kingdom to sustain this ambition, and pay for it, entailed a steady increase in royal power and authority.

Under Richelieu, taxes rose inexorably, office-holders were ruthlessly manipulated, and intendants extensively deployed for the first time to enforce the king's will in the provinces. Richelieu also resisted the claims of the higher nobility to participate by right in central government, and undermined their provincial authority with a network of clients dependent on his own patronage. Mazarin, who succeeded to his power and prolonged his policies, was the most successful of these.

Unsurprisingly, Richelieu was widely hated and feared. But his principles and example set a pattern for much that Louis XIV and his ministers would do. One of the king's favourite jokes was that his minister Colbert was always advising him to do "what the great Cardinal would have done". ■

borrowing from the wealthiest groups at court or in the capital, and then bolstered their credit by buying financial offices, and by living in ostentatious luxury. Since their main business was extracting money, *traitants* were widely hated and demonised as public bloodsuckers.

Even worse, acting under contract with the king, they could call upon his officers to enforce their authority. Under Richelieu there had been a proliferation of these so-called intendants: all-powerful crown commissioners sent into the provinces, supposedly to "find out all injustices and oppressions that the king's subjects might suffer from officers and ministers of justice through corruption, negligence, ignorance or otherwise, in whatever way or manner, and all contraventions of

VENAL OFFICE

Since the early 16th century the crown had raised money by selling public positions and manipulating privileges attached to them. Venality was a thinly disguised way of borrowing: having once bought an office from the king, the holder could be blackmailed into paying out further sums to maintain or increase his privileges. The highest offices conferred nobility, but normally only after three generations. It was therefore essential to be able to pass them on within the family, which was guaranteed by the payment of an annual due or *paulette*, introduced in 1604 and subject to periodic renewal.

By the accession of Louis XIII there were perhaps 25,000 venal offices, comprising the whole judiciary and a range of financial and administrative functions. The

the laws". In reality, they did far more to enforce tax demands than to protect the poor from extortion.

Intendants remained a mainstay of government under Mazarin, and everybody detested them. Even the great magnates governing the provinces resented them, as they were rival representatives of the king's authority. Above all they were abominated by venal office-holders, whose privileges, revenues, and jurisdictions were threatened by their wide and ill-defined powers.

Office-holders at every level had been relentlessly squeezed under Richelieu, from the lowest petty jurisdictions up to the sovereign courts of appeal (the parlements). They all hoped the pressure would ease with the new reign. The leading system continued to expand after France entered the Thirty Years' War, and in the 1630s it was bringing in between 25 and 40 per cent of the crown's annual revenue. While selling hereditary judicial offices was widely recognised as undesirable, the system could only be ended by reimbursing all the office-holders. From the time of Richelieu onwards this was widely recognised as impossibly expensive.

Venality gave judges tenure, and from that a certain ability to influence royal policies. But it also made them ultimately more dependent on the king than on the patronage of great nobles. Richelieu, who had begun his career denouncing venality, came to think it was a necessary evil.

Under Mazarin the number of venal offices continued to expand, reaching over 45,000 by 1664, with a capital value of 420,000,000 livres. But the discontents of over-exploited venal magistrates were the trigger for the Fronde. ∎

court in the kingdom, the parlement of Paris, began with a gesture of goodwill. The very first act of the widowed queen was to ask the magistrates to overturn her husband's will, which limited her powers as regent. The parlement had endorsed the will only a few weeks earlier, but in a solemn act of sovereign power (*lit de justice*) in the presence of the boy king they agreed to recognise her full royal authority until her son came of age.

Did Mazarin overplay his hand?

Nothing else changed, however. The war went on, and the privileges, powers and incomes of office-holders continued to be encroached on by Particelli and swarming *traitants*. Provincial officers and courts were exploited even more rapaciously than those of Paris. New or increased taxes, which had to be registered in the parlements to take effect, were forced through in *lits de justice* despite their protests. Mazarin, meanwhile, flaunted his growing wealth just as Richelieu had done. "The greatness and even the good of great princes," the latter had complacently told Louis XIII, "is ordinarily that those who have the leading positions in their states and are most in their confidence should make a goodly fortune." By the time he died, Mazarin was even richer than his notorious role model.

Yet in 1648 he overreached himself. To ease the registration of more contentious legislation, the magistrates in the Parisian courts had been spared some of the more extortionate charges imposed on venal office-holders. Now, to fund a final push to secure peace in the German negotiations, the way in which magistrates were able to hold on to their offices was threatened. The crown refused to renew the *paulette,* the tax guaranteeing free disposal and heredity of offices, for its normal nine years unless officers sacrificed some of their value. To secure registration, the magistrates of the parlement were exempted. Divide and rule had always been the way to exploit office-holders most effectively; but this time the ploy failed.

All the Parisian courts united to resist the new demands. In June 1648 their representatives met in the St. Louis Chamber of the parlement, and, in defiance of the regent, issued a 27-point manifesto, a comprehensive indictment of the way the kingdom had been governed since the time of Richelieu. It demanded the withdrawal of intendants, the cancellation of contracts with *traitants,* and a cut of a quarter in direct taxes. It called for a special "chamber of justice" to investigate and punish suspected frauds by *traitants.*

All new taxes, it declared, should be subject to the consent of the sovereign courts – no more *lits de justice* – and so should manipulations of venal offices. The more notorious manipulations were to be banned. The royal council should also be unable to override the judgements of sovereign courts, and arbitrary imprisonments should be prohibited. Various claims to regulate trade and prices in the capital were added to this heterogeneous list, reflecting the magistrates' awareness that their stand was winning widespread popular support in the capital.

Triggered by the programme of the St. Louis Chamber, there was a huge outburst of unregulated pamphleteering. By 1653 there were more than 5000 *mazarinades*, discussing every aspect of what developed into a five-year crisis in the French state. Bowing to this upsurge of opposition, Mazarin dismissed and exiled Particelli. All this achieved was to send a wave of panic through the community of financiers and *traitants*, and the crown's credit

LIT DE JUSTICE

Magistrates in the parlements and other sovereign courts dispensed justice in the king's name, and the most important laws only came into force when these courts "registered" them by transcribing them into their official records.

Before registration, the magistrates were entitled to point out problems or defects in the laws by sending the king remonstrances. By this means they could delay and obstruct new legislation. But the king was the fount of all justice, and if he came in person to the court there was no technical need for magistrates to represent him.

Laws could then be registered by his direct order without any remonstrances. The ceremony at which this took place was called a *lit de justice*. It was a rare occurrence, but was normally the final word on even the most contentious matters, a supreme act of royal sovereignty. When the king was a minor, however, there were doubts about the legitimacy of imposing legislation by this means, since a regent was not a true sovereign. ∎

abruptly dried up. After several weeks of agonised temporising, the queen and her minister were forced to accept the officers' demands. The state apparatus as it had evolved during the war seemed on the verge of collapse.

The boy-king witnessed all this in silence. At *lits de justice* he delivered formulaic words; he followed the regular religious observances prescribed by his devout Spanish mother; but nobody knew what he was thinking. The Prince de Condé considered him a fool, which mattered little while he was still a minor, but his legal majority was now only three years away.

What caused the first Fronde, and how did it end?

The grievances set out by the Parisian courts in the St. Louis Chamber echoed complaints that their provincial counterparts had been raising for over a decade. The news from Paris encouraged renewed outbursts of protests from courts and office-holders all over the kingdom. But no sooner had the regent and Mazarin accepted the demands of the magistracy than news of a victory by Condé over the Spaniards at Lens (20th August 1648) encouraged them to strike back. The queen ordered the arrest of Broussel, the most eloquent and determined spokesman of judicial resistance in the parlement.

It was a serious miscalculation. Broussel enjoyed widespread popularity, and barricades sprang up all over the city in support of the parlement. Surrounded by hostile crowds in the Palais Royal, she was compelled to rescind the arrest. Over the last months of 1648 the parlement dictated events in the capital, and once again the regent accepted the demands of the St. Louis Chamber, even though this involved, as Mazarin privately observed, abolishing the best part of the monarchy.

It was perhaps better, however, than risking the destruction of monarchy itself, as was happening at that very moment in England, to the horror of French onlookers. And soon there was fresh hope for the queen and the cardinal in the signature of the Peace of Westphalia in Germany, and the return of Condé from his triumphs on the battlefield to take the lead in quelling the rebellious capital.

To clear the way for an assault, it was decided to remove the king to safety, and on the night of 5th January 1649 he and his mother made a secret dash to Saint-Germain. He did not return to Paris for eight months, and the memory of this flight from his own subjects marked Louis XIV for life. It was his first introduction to serious monarchical politics.

Condé laid siege to the city, where a number of rival magnates as well as the populace rallied initially to the magistrates. But the deprivations of living under blockade soon sapped popular confidence, and within weeks the parlement was offering to negotiate a truce. A renewed Spanish offensive from the Netherlands alarmed all sides while, belatedly, the provincial seats of some parlements, like Aix and Bordeaux, were inspired to revolt by the Parisian example. Rebels everywhere called for the dismissal of Mazarin, but this was one concession the queen would not make. As the price of Parisian surrender she confirmed her previous acceptance of most of the magistrates' original demands, but when the king rode triumphantly back into the capital in August 1649, her cardinal was with him.

Thus ended the first rebellion, or Fronde* ("the Fronde of the Magistrates") – although in Bordeaux it flickered on until 1653 as the Ormée. That city's rebellion was sustained by a new outbreak of civil war from the beginning of 1650. Condé, who thought his blockade of Paris had saved the monarchy, expected to be rewarded with the leading role in the state; but Mazarin still stood in the way. A proud prince of the blood, Condé despised this foreign upstart, but his own arrogance alienated a number of leading magnates who might have supported him. Parisians, too – now led by their archbishop designate, de Retz – never forgot *Monsieur le Prince*'s role in starving them out.

Relying on Condé's unpopularity, the queen and the cardinal ordered his arrest in January 1650. Just as the arrest of Broussel had triggered the first Fronde, that of Condé set off a second. Unlike Broussel, the prince remained imprisoned for a

---

* The Frondes were named after the slings which were used by rebels to smash windows.

year, but his kingdom-wide network of clients and 'creatures' exploded into defiance. They even showed themselves open to offers of support from Spain. The regent reacted with a desperate series of military campaigns, usually accompanied by the king. Everywhere the royal presence embarrassed and intimidated rebels, who always claimed that the real object of their defiance was not the king but Mazarin.

By early 1651, hatred of the cardinal was once more widespread in Paris. A second planned flight of the queen and her son was thwarted by a mob demanding to see their king – another terrifying memory to haunt him. This time they were not refugees, but prisoners of the capital.

Mazarin, waiting in vain outside the city to welcome them to safety, now sought to appease Condé by releasing him from captivity. The prince went disdainfully to Paris to resume his governmental claims, lending his authority to a chorus of demands for an end to the rule of the foreign favourite.

Mazarin gave way. He went into exile in Germany, although continuing to correspond in secret with the queen. But his withdrawal proved a masterstroke, since hostility to him was the main cement holding the frondeurs together. His departure revealed that they had no other agreed aims. By careful manipulation and redistribution of royal patronage the queen divided their leaders. Her clear objective was to temporise until

September 1651, when her son reached 13.

It was a wise move. As soon as the king reached his majority, everything changed. Although the young king remained for some time largely the mouthpiece of his mother and the cardinal, it was no longer possible for rebels to claim that royal authority was being usurped. Lavish ceremonies in Paris marked the majority, and, for the first time, Louis XIV danced and gambled in public. Every major figure in the kingdom was present – with the exception of Condé.

How were the rebels finally defeated?

With the queen's authority as regent at an end, Condé decided to seize power for himself by force. Once more he organised his extensive clientele of governors and military captains for rebellion. Now he openly accepted offers of help from Spain. All this gave Mazarin the excuse he needed to return from exile with an army, ostensibly to defend the king from his traitor cousin. Yet his reappearance was enough to drive other royal princes such as Gaston d'Orléans on to Condé's side. The second Fronde became the "Fronde of the Princes", a brutal civil war.

The king was kept at the forefront of his own forces, although he now also relied on the leadership of Turenne, Condé's equal as a general, but hitherto unpredictable in his loyalties. In 1652, despite this,

Condé's armies captured Paris, where his soldiers ran amok. They then found themselves in a trap: royal forces surrounded the capital while systematically subduing the princes' provincial centres of support.

Once again, all that held the frondeurs together was hatred of Mazarin. He unlocked the situation in the summer of 1652 by a second withdrawal from the court, though this time only to a distant frontier. Again it worked. Support for the princes melted away. Retz, a key rebel leader, was won over when Mazarin secured him a cardinal's hat. Paris began to clamour for the king's return. On 14th October Condé and his entourage left for the Spanish Netherlands and spent the next seven years in the service of King Philip IV.

A week later Louis XIV re-entered his capital in triumph, acclaimed by the populace as the restorer of peace. At a *lit de justice* the next day a general amnesty for all but a few of the leading frondeurs was proclaimed. The parlement was forbidden to intervene in affairs of state, including financial matters. Gaston d'Orléans was sent into provincial exile; Retz was arrested by the king in person; and, in February 1653, Mazarin finally reappeared at the monarch's side as his principal minister. Parisian defiance was at an end, and the restoration of provincial calm was crowned by the surrender of Bordeaux in July.

The five years of upheaval and intermittent civil war since 1648 had also been marked by disastrous harvests in 1651 and 1652, outbreaks of plague, and the indiscriminate ravages of unpaid soldiers living off the land. The memory of these horrors produced a deep and universal longing for order and security, fundamental to understanding why the confident personal rule of Louis XIV was later so readily accepted.

Not that any frondeur had ever questioned the king's authority. The fate of Charles I of England, executed in 1649, appalled everybody. (He had been married to the king's aunt.) But the authority of the regent during a minority had never been beyond dispute from princes of the blood in line for the throne, and especially when the regent's chief minister was a wily foreigner. And when, to pay for an unpopular war, this contested government relied on a range of extortionate fiscal blackmail, the apparatus of the state cracked under the strain.

Yet there was no revolutionary movement, and no long-term unity among the varied groups opposed to Mazarin and what he stood for. Even before the king came of age they were repeatedly at odds with each other, their quarrels periodically reducing the kingdom to anarchy. Taxpayers, it is true, benefited fleetingly from the Fronde through the temporary inability of the state to enforce its demands. But the only permanent beneficiary was the monarch himself, who learnt from hard experience what could happen in a kingdom where nobody was in undisputed control.

What steps did Mazarin take to prepare the monarch for power?

Although the Peace of Westphalia had ended the war in Germany, the war with Spain went on. And the threat from Spain was far more serious than the threat from Germany had been. Spanish territories ringed France, and, with peace on the Rhine, Spain was able to concentrate its forces against France alone.

The continuing war was a major grievance among the frondeurs, and Mazarin's overriding ambition, warmly supported by the queen mother, was now to achieve a durable peace with her brother, the king of Spain. This called for a renewed war effort, and paying for it meant reactivating many of the "extraordinary" expedients which had provoked the Fronde in the first place.

But at least the minority was over. Mazarin took care to promote the king in all his glory at every opportunity. In 1654 Louis XIV was at last crowned and anointed with great ceremony in the traditional setting of Rheims cathedral. From then on, he appeared whenever possible with his armies on campaign, observing the sieges and battles conducted in his name. He regularly attended meetings of the council of state, where the major decisions were taken. And in private the cardinal gradually introduced him to every aspect of the techniques of ruling.

Mazarin knew that his own position depended

Portrait of cardinal Jules Mazarin

on keeping the king close, and, when the young monarch fell gravely ill in 1658, he prepared himself for disgrace and exile. But, once recovered, the monarch continued to be utterly supportive of his godfather and mentor. His loyalty lasted until the day Mazarin's death finally brought the king freedom to govern by all the maxims he had been taught.

Meanwhile, the cardinal became even richer than Richelieu. He built himself a lavish mansion crammed with expensive works of art. He left enough money in his will to endow a vast new college for the education of scholars from the four new provinces added to the kingdom while he was principal minister. He made sure that his Italian relatives married into the higher ranks of the French nobility – although he drew the line at allowing Louis XIV to marry his first love, Mazarin's own niece Marie Mancini. A king's hand was too precious an asset to be wasted in a non-dynastic match.

The queen mother hoped that peace with Spain could be sealed by her son marrying his cousin, the Infanta Maria Teresa; but when this was suggested to Philip IV in 1656 the Spanish king refused, preferring a match with his Austrian Habsburg cousins. Mazarin's objective was to force him to change his mind.

Meanwhile the powers and practices which had helped trigger the Fronde – and which the regency had promised to abandon – were steadily resumed. Intendants reappeared where they had been withdrawn. *Traitants* re-emerged to propose new ways of raising money, and nothing was done to set up the promised tribunal to investigate their profiteering. The idea of tax cuts was tacitly abandoned, and the parlements were forbidden to discuss financial matters.

When, in 1655, the parlement of Paris tried to "examine" a new batch of fiscal edicts, the king strode abruptly into its deliberations. Declaring that "everybody knows how much trouble your meetings have caused my State and the dangerous results they have produced", he explicitly forbade

Mazarin's College of Four Nations, now the Institut de France

the magistrates to discuss finance. They continued to grumble, but the crown now took good care not to squeeze office-holders as ruthlessly as before 1648. Few new offices were created, and the *paulette* was renewed without extorting extra payment.

Another reason for the relative acquiescence of the parlement was that its second most important officer, the procurator-general Nicolas Fouquet, was, for the first time in its history, also the superintendant of the king's finances. Fouquet had not always supported Mazarin, but he knew how to handle the world of finance – and how to enjoy the rewards of office. His management of taxation produced a substantial rise in revenues, and he was able to negotiate crucial loans at key moments in the war. He clearly saw himself as a potential first minister after Mazarin, and over a decade he built up a far-reaching network of clients.

He had several well-entrenched rivals, however. There was Hugues de Lionne, a diplomat at the heart of every important negotiation, and Michel Le Tellier, an experienced military administrator and secretary of state for war. Years earlier, Le Tellier had recommended to Mazarin the services of a young assistant, Jean-Baptiste Colbert, who by the early 1650s was managing the cardinal's immense fortune, and remained in Mazarin's personal service throughout the next decade. From 1659 Colbert anxiously watched his ageing patron's health begin to fail. He had every reason to fear that when Mazarin died the widespread hatred of the Italian would be directed at clients like himself – unless he could win the support of the king.

With the tax holiday of the Fronde now over – and a renewed war effort against Spain – there were soon fresh signs of unrest in many parts of the kingdom. Assemblies of noblemen in western districts complained of the erosion of their privileges. There were several minor peasant tax revolts; and in 1658 the whole of Provence was thrown into turmoil by additional war levies. The port of Marseille came out in open defiance of royal authority.

It was a fraught moment, but the war was at last turning in France's favour. As ruthless as Richelieu in befriending Protestant heretics, and setting aside Bourbon support for the exiled Stuarts, Mazarin made an alliance with Cromwell's British Republic.* With the support of Britain's navy and troops, Turenne (as Louis XIV himself looked on) defeated a Spanish army led by Condé at the battle of the Dunes (14th June 1658). Simultaneously, Mazarin opened negotiations for the king to marry an Italian princess of the House of Savoy. The move was designed to panic the defeated Philip IV into ending the war by offering his daughter's hand to the French king. It worked. Over the summer the two kingdoms thrashed out terms which, in November, became the Peace of the Pyrenees.

To his mother's delight, Louis XIV was now at last betrothed to the Infanta Maria Teresa – the most eligible (though scarcely the most attractive) princess in Europe. Just as the queen mother, when she herself was an Infanta, had married Louis XIII, the new consort, Maria Teresa, renounced all claims to inherit the throne of Spain – although French acceptance of this was conditional on the payment of a dowry which Mazarin rightly suspected would never materialise. Meanwhile, France acquired from Spain Artois in the north, Roussillon in the south, and various strategic enclaves along the eastern frontier. Condé was allowed to return unpunished, but the only

---

* Following the end of the Civil War and the execution of Charles I in 1649 Britain was ruled as a republic. At first power lay with parliament and the council of state, but between 1653 and the restoration of the monarchy in 1660 the country was ruled by Oliver Cromwell, a fervent Protestant, and then, briefly, by his son Richard.

The infanta Maria Theresa aged 14 *by Diego Velázquez*

substantial concession made by France was to stop helping Portuguese rebels against King Philip.

The marriage was solemnised in 1660 on the Basque frontier between the two kingdoms. From there the royal couple travelled eastwards to Marseille, where the city meekly surrendered to the king at the head of his troops. With enemies at home and abroad now vanquished, Louis XIV and his bride progressed north to Paris to make, on 26th August, a lavish ceremonial entry, the first (and last) of his reign.

Mazarin was too ill to join a procession

celebrating the triumph of all his policies and, just over six months later, he was dead. On the day after he died, Louis XIV summoned Séguier the chancellor, the senior official of the crown, along with Fouquet, Le Tellier, Lionne and other secretaries of state. He told them he intended to govern by himself. They were to advise him when asked, but were to sign and authorise nothing without his express permission. They found it hard to believe, and most courtiers thought this royal resolution could not last. But, as the king later recalled, "the world did not yet know me". Government by first ministers, much less cardinals, was at an end. The mature Louis XIV was determined to rule as well as reign.

How have historians judged the first reign?

Historical discussion of Louis XIV begins with an old and powerful argument, often called the *thèse royale*. This holds that from the 16th century down to the French Revolution, the monarchy and its agents were engaged in building a centralised, authoritarian state of increasing efficiency and rationality, a system of "absolutism". Pioneered under Richelieu and Mazarin, absolute monarchy reached its peak when Louis XIV took personal control in 1661.

Historians taking this view have never doubted

the legitimacy of absolute monarchy, whether as a matter of law or practical necessity, seeing the alternative as anarchy. Making absolutism work, they argue, involved a constant struggle against nobles, whether great magnates or ennobled office-holders, who constantly sought to protect or expand their own power and privileges, selfishly indifferent to the wider interests of the kingdom. The higher nobility and parlements were irresponsible in holding the monarchy to ransom at a time when it was involved in a desperate struggle against the Habsburgs. Their obstruction and

---

TITLES AND MOTTOES

Most Christian King or *Roi très-chrétien*, the official style of the French king since the late Middle Ages.

King of France and Navarre Louis XIV's grandfather, Henry IV, founder of the Bourbon dynasty, had been king of Navarre, a small Pyrenean principality, before succeeding to the French throne in 1589. He chose to keep his two titles separate, as did his heirs. The royal coat of arms always displayed the insignia of both kingdoms together.

Sun King or *Roi Soleil*. A description adopted by Louis XIV in 1662, possibly to outshine the title "Planet King" used by the King of Spain to reflect his worldwide dominions. He was often depicted (and sometimes danced) as Apollo, the Greek sun god, and images of the sun were used everywhere in official royal decoration. The sun, he wrote, "by its unique quality, by the way it shines, by the light which it sheds on the other stars which form a sort of court around it, by the equal

defiance seemed to justify all that Louis XIV later did to rein them in.

The influential modern historian Roland Mousnier made this case succinctly in a Historical Association pamphlet, *Louis XIV* (1973); (so, more recently, did François Bluche), while the most recent leading advocate of the view writing in English is Richard Bonney.

But what were the nobles defying? None of them dreamed of overthrowing the monarchy; and so long as the king was a minor, royal authority was in abeyance and the kingdom was governed by

---

and just sharing of this same light among all the diverse climes of the world, by the good which it does in all places, constantly producing life, joy and action on all sides, by its unceasing movement, appearing nevertheless always calm, by that constant and invariable course, from which it never departs or varies, is surely the most vivid and finest image of a great monarch".

Louis the Great or *Louis le Grand*. A title offered to the king by the City of Paris in 1671. Ministers encouraged its general use during the triumphant 1670s and 80s, but it scarcely survived his reign. Its last echo is in the name of one of the most prestigious *lycées* in Paris.

Nec Pluribus Impar, "not unequal to many", the king's official motto from 1662, by which, he wrote "was intended what agreeably flattered the ambition of a young king, that, capable alone of so many things, I would doubtless be further capable of governing other empires, as the sun would light up other worlds, if they were equally exposed to its rays". The idea that the king of France could contemplate adding other kingdoms to his dominions naturally alarmed his neighbours. ■

unpopular foreigners – a Spanish queen and her Italian favourite who had failed to end Richelieu's war and the unprecedented fiscal demands which it had brought. But studied up close these now seem more like a series of hand-to-mouth expedients than a deliberate programme of state-building. Their effect was to provoke popular rebellions and to alienate the elites, who otherwise saw themselves as natural partners of the crown in governing the kingdom. The Fronde, in this light, was an explosion of understandable resentments.

On this basis, "revisionist" historians have argued that France could not be effectively governed without the co-operation of the social and institutional elites, and the networks of patronage through which they operated. Absolute in theory the monarchy might have been, but in practice it had to compromise with its leading subjects. As William H. Beik, one of the founders of (English-language) revisionism, concluded: "Under Louis XIV it was perfectly clear that hierarchy would be reinforced, the claims of the privileged to their share of society's resources would be guaranteed, and collaboration would be properly rewarded."*

---

* *Absolutism and Society in seventeenth century France*, p. 334.

THE SECOND REIGN, 1660s-1680s: power and glory

How did the king establish his personal authority?

A new pattern of government did not emerge overnight. The only hint of things to come on the day after Mazarin died was that Nicolas Fouquet, the superintendent of the king's finances, was instructed to work with Jean-Baptiste Colbert, who had been Mazarin's manager. In fact, Colbert had been privately denouncing the superintendent's financial conduct for two years, and Fouquet knew it. What he did not realise was how seriously the king took Colbert's criticisms, which alleged that he had systematically enriched himself at royal expense.

Shortly after paying a visit to the superintendent's newly-built country estate at Vaux-le-Vicomte, the king resolved to arrest him. Fouquet's lifestyle was scarcely more luxurious than Richelieu's or Mazarin's had been, and he was nothing like as rich; but the king's mind had been made up. The office of superintendent was suppressed, and Fouquet was put on trial before a special "chamber of justice". It sat for three years, but the hand-picked judges could not agree on a unanimous verdict. They ignored a royal hint that the accused deserved to die, but when they merely sentenced him to banishment, the king changed the penalty to life imprisonment. Fouquet languished in jail until he died in 1680.

Also brought to trial before the chamber of justice were the leading *traitants* with whom the superintendent had dealt so successfully, accused (as the frondeurs had demanded years earlier) of extortion, embezzlement and profiteering since 1635. Some were condemned to death or banishment, but most were only heavily fined. Making these notorious "leeches" and "bloodsuckers" cough up (*rendre gorge*) brought the king widespread popularity – although throughout his reign he was never able to do without their services.

It was Fouquet's spectacular public downfall which notified the world that the king was really serious in his determination to rule for himself, with no first minister. Forty years later, advising his grandson on how to be a king in Spain, Louis XIV set out succinctly the principles of ruling from which he had never wavered: "Do not let yourself be governed; be the master; never have either favourites or a first minister; listen to, consult, your Council, but you decide." As he told an overconfident Colbert in 1671: "Do not risk vexing me ... because after I have heard your arguments and those of your colleagues, and have given my opinion ... I do not wish ever to hear of it further ... after a decision I give you I wish no word of reply."

Portrait of Louis XIV of France (1638–1715)

The council was always kept small, and nobody sat there as of right, unlike the princes and magnates who had claimed seats on the council of regency. In fact they were now deliberately excluded in favour of men of less elevated rank. "I had above all to establish my own reputation," the king informed his son,

> and to let the public know, by the very rank from which I took them, that my intention was not to share my authority with them. It was important to me that they did not themselves conceive

higher hopes than it pleased me to give them: which is difficult for people of high birth.

Whom did he rely on to help him?

Ministers were not, however, newcomers or nonentities. The king chose men he knew, "a small number whom chance presents us with", and he repaid their loyalty with his own. Throughout his rule he relied on successive generations of a handful of families – the Le Telliers, the Colberts, the Phélypeaux. He made them rich (though never on the scale of the cardinals or Fouquet), heaped them with patronage, and saw their daughters married into more aristocratic families. But he never raised them to the level of the peerage. Not only would that have given them independent status, it would also have outraged the highest ranks of the nobility, who were granted power in other ways.

Louis XIV was not anti-aristocratic. Proud to be the "first gentleman of his kingdom", his tastes were those of any great nobleman: making war, hunting, ostentatious display of his rank, dynastic pride. Apart from servants, noble courtiers were the only people he ever met. And they were the only ones he thought fit to hold high honorific offices, or to represent his person as provincial governors or in command of armies.

To qualify for these prestigious and lucrative appointments, however, they had to be noticed by the king. They had to be at court, to attend on the royal household where lay the source of all honours and privileges. But if they were at court, dancing (often quite literally) attendance on the king, they could not be on the provincial lands which had served so many of them as semi-independent power-bases over the preceding century. Louis XIV did not, as often used to be said, denude the provinces of nobility by insisting that they live at court. No court could have accommodated all 240,000 nobles. But he did surround himself with several hundred of the more important princes and magnates, *les grands* as they came to be known, making them absentees from their provinces for much of the time, and leaving everyday social and institutional authority to lesser nobles.

Provincial governors, great magnates still, remained key figures of influence, although now only occasionally resident in their provinces and appointed for a mere three years at a time. But the crown's permanent provincial agents were once again the hated intendants. Like the ministers to whom they reported, intendants were not of the highest birth, coming mainly from the Parisian robe nobility. Their tenure was as precarious as that of their ministerial patrons. And although their powers were far-reaching and open-ended, their everyday effectiveness ultimately depended on the cooperation of local elites – magistrates of the sovereign courts, or officials of the estates.

Such groups, rich in provincial terms, had been

mercilessly squeezed since 1635, and their patience had snapped in the Fronde. But those upheavals had taught them that, however rapacious and extortionate royal authority, without its underpinning there was no security for their own privileges. Once the young king, free of his unpopular Italian mentor, asserted his prerogatives, they were reluctant to defy him again; just as he, with his own alarming memories of the Fronde, took care not to push these essential servants too far by undermining their position on their home territory.

Nonetheless, it is true that Louis XIV thought the parlements had presumed too much during his minority, and must be brought to heel. In 1673 they were told that they might only submit remonstrances *after* registration of unwelcome legislation, and not before. Remonstrances, they would be told by ministers later in the reign, were no longer in fashion. "But I protest to you sincerely", the king told his son, "that I have … neither aversion nor bitterness in my mind towards my officers of justice. On the contrary, if age is venerable in men, it seems to me even more so in bodies as old as these. I am convinced that in no other part of the state is the work perhaps harder, or rewards fewer."

Louis XIV respected hard work in others, because it was a duty he imposed upon himself. As to work, he wrote, "it is through it that you reign, and you reign for that". He believed, too, in recognising and rewarding loyalty. But in return he expected unquestioning obedience. To achieve all he wished, he declared, "the first foundation was to make my will quite absolute, through conduct which imposed submission and respect". Absolute monarchy meant nothing more than this to the king, although theorists were always ready with more elaborate rationales.

The sovereign's decisions were final. He knew he was expected, as the fount of all justice in his kingdom, to uphold and abide by the law. But if he did not, nobody was entitled to resist or defy him. Nobody but God might call him to account. But

DUELS

Settling private quarrels by single combat had a long history but, involving as it did the killing of one of the participants, it was condemned by the church. Civil legislation also outlawed duelling, and the king of France at his coronation swore an oath never to pardon those involved.

Nevertheless, duels were common, especially among noblemen and soldiers, as repeated prohibitions show. Richelieu brought a renewed determination to eliminating a practice which he thought damaged the nobility and deprived the king of warriors, and in 1627 he had one of the more notorious noble duellists publicly executed.

The anarchy of the Fronde years saw a resurgence, but Louis XIV, too, thought duelling a sign of indiscipline and lawlessness. Not even the defence of noble honour entitled men to flout the king's law. A comprehensive prohibition was issued in 1679, in which the king took special pride. Duelling was not eliminated, but became less common. Whether this was because of stricter enforcement of the law, or because of changing social values, remains a moot point. ■

Louis XIV was not a capricious tyrant. He ruled as a methodical bureaucrat, for whom kingship was a craft (*métier*). His instinct was to abide by existing laws and customs rather than to flout or override them. He knew that this was what his subjects wanted, and that it was the way to secure their co-operation in his pursuit of the glory befitting a great king.

How did the king impose his authority on France?

A confident and consistent approach to government was one thing; making it work was another. The unquestioned authority which the king sought could be imposed only gradually.

The first few years of personal rule coincided with widespread famine. There were revolts in

ABSOLUTISM

Nobody spoke of "absolutism" until the 19th century, but absolute monarchy was an idea well understood in the 17th. It meant a monarchy whose subjects had no share in the exercise of sovereign power and no right of resistance. It did not mean a monarchy free to ignore or change the laws of the kingdom at will: it was those very laws that gave kings their thrones, and arbitrary government meant tyranny.

Louis XIV has often been depicted as the archetypal absolute monarch, and it is true that he thought no subject had the right to resist his authority. He believed that he had been chosen to rule by God, and that several regions where the return of peace had not brought the expected fall in taxation. Episodic rural unrest continued throughout the 1660s, and became more serious in the subsequent decade when a major war was financed with a new series of "extraordinary" expedients. Bordeaux, and then much of Brittany, defied royal authority for weeks in 1675, and the local parlements failed (perhaps deliberately) to restore order. It took thousands of troops billeted in rebel cities to do so. The delinquent parlements were punished by years of exile in little towns remote from their usual seats in provincial capitals. Only after these convulsions did open defiance of the crown fade away.

Large numbers of regular troops were not available for much of the 1660s. By 1665, after six years of peace, the king had around 50,000 regular soldiers, but most of them were assigned to the

---

to resist the king was to resist the divine will. Resistance in any case risked anarchy, as the first years of his own reign seemed to prove.

But his way of ruling was anything but arbitrary, whether in dealing with legislation or in day-to-day decision-making. He governed through lawyers, backed efforts to improve and codify legislation, and took care to observe established customs and procedures. That his mature rule encountered so little resistance reflected his subjects' relief that the uncertain times of mid-century were now over – they had a confident king who knew how to rule. Few regarded their absolute monarch as a tyrant.

Only in the last two years of the reign was their confidence shaken as he tinkered with the law of succession and invited the Pope to interfere in the kingdom's affairs. ■

security of the frontiers, and could only be drawn on by the civil power in emergencies. Direct royal authority over France's 20 million subjects, in what was the largest kingdom in western Europe, was entrusted to no more than 300 royal appointees, including intendants, their subdelegates, and the staff of ministries. To enforce their orders there were a few thousand mounted police. Thus there was little alternative to co-operation with the tenured holders of venal offices, most of whom were judges of one sort or another.

Jean-Baptiste Colbert, appointed in 1665 to the new post of comptroller-general of the finances, was unhappy about this dependence. Since 1659 he

---

LOUIS XIV IN HIS OWN WORDS

L'Etat c'est moi ("I am the state"). Reputedly said at the *lit de justice* of 14th April 1655, but there is no direct record of it. The young king, still in tutelage to Mazarin, simply reproved the magistrates for resisting new fiscal edicts. On his deathbed, in fact, he declared "I am leaving, but the State remains".

In his *Memoirs*, addressed to his son: "The craft of kingship (*métier de roi*) is grand, noble and delicious, when one feels worthy of performing well all the things it requires; but it is not without its pains, fatigue, and worries."

"To increase their own greatness is the most worthy and agreeable occupation of sovereigns." (*Memoirs*)

"Pay great attention to business; in discussing it, start by listening at length before deciding... always hear out all the opinions and arguments of your council, before making a decision." (*Memoirs*)

"Of all sovereign functions,

had been urging Mazarin and then the young king to diminish the number of offices, and cut back the privileges and remuneration which went with them. Colbert disapproved of the the sale of offices, thinking that it diverted investment away from more productive activity and enabled many of the king's richer subjects to dodge paying direct taxes. By 1670 he claimed to have abolished 20,000 useless offices. But the financial demands of the Dutch War thwarted his ambition of eliminating venality entirely, and by the time he died in 1683 all the ways of wringing money out of office-holders had been fully deployed again. Venality, it seemed, was too useful to do without.

---

management of the finances is the one of which a prince should be most jealous." (*Memoirs*)

To Colbert, November 1671: "Think about it. If you can't do it, there will always be someone who can."

"Nothing is forgiven to those of our rank." (*Memoirs*)

On the offer of the Spanish Succession in 1700: "I am sure that whatever I decide to do, many people will blame me."

Rejecting allied peace terms in 1710: "I can say that I went against my character and that I did myself extreme violence to secure prompt repose to my subjects at the expense of my reputation or at least of my own satisfaction, and perhaps of my glory that I was willing to risk for the advantage of those through whom I acquired it: I thought I owed them that acknowledgement."

To the future Louis XV, on his deathbed: "Try to keep the peace with your neighbours. I have loved war too much; do not imitate me in this, or in the too great sums I have spent ... Bring relief to your people as soon as you can, and do what I have had the misfortune not to be able to do myself." ∎

Colbert thought the only subjects worthy of a king, apart from soldiers and sailors, were productive workers in agriculture and industry. Wherever possible he sought to diminish privileges which took anyone out of such employment. He was also convinced that many tax-avoidance privileges could not be justified. Along with his assaults on venality he launched inquiries into nobility (*recherches de noblesse*), which examined the lineage of supposedly noble families to ensure they were as ancient as they claimed.

So far from anti-noble, this policy was popular with older families who deplored the adulteration of their ranks by ambitious upstarts. But, like the reforms to venality, it scarcely survived the search for immediate profits in times of war. By the 1690s the king was routinely selling new patents of nobility, and then blackmailing their acquirers with revocation unless they paid for periodic "confirmations". Most grants of privilege, in fact, originated in monarchical weakness. But once established, privileges as an emergency resource could be made to yield far more than if their holders had remained subject to ordinary taxation.

Unable then, and in many ways unwilling, to interfere with the structure of society or its venalised institutions of power, royal authority had to impose itself in less coercive ways. Throughout the 1660s, largely under the impetus of Colbert but with the king's enthusiastic support, substantial sums were spent to glorify God's anointed ruler. Writers and artists were subsidised to sing his praises and depict his achievements. Academies of Sciences, Inscriptions, Music and Architecture were established under royal patronage, and eminent foreigners were lured to Paris by offers of pensions, amid hints that they should proclaim their gratitude.*

Even before he became comptroller-general, Colbert was made superintendent of royal buildings (1664) and oversaw an ambitious programme to refurbish royal palaces. "Your majesty knows," he reminded the king, "that with the exception of brilliant military actions nothing speaks so eloquently of the greatness and wisdom of princes as buildings." Louis XIV did know, and it was his own decision in 1668 to begin extending his father's hunting lodge at Versailles into a palace to outshine anything a subject might afford. Versailles would be a building site until four years before he died, and none of it was fit for occupation until 1682. But its vast scale, lavish gardens and decoration, and the glittering court it housed, proclaimed the power and glory of the King of France on a scale that no other monarch could match – although many would try over the next century.

Colbert understood, and taught the king, that costly display ought to be paid for from the taxable wealth of his subjects, which should be increased by economic stimulus. Colbert measured the kingdom's wealth in precious metals, and thought

---

* A pension was a regular payment made to an artist or scholar to encourage them to carry out work of value to the crown.

that the quantity of them in the world was limited, so the French could only increase their share at others' expense. They should buy as little and sell as much abroad as possible.

This meant, above all, manufacturing high-value luxury goods which rich people would buy, such as furniture, mirrors, tapestries and fine cloth. Royal manufactories were established, with lavish privileges and subsidies, to outshine and outsell foreign competitors. The prime targets were the Dutch, the greatest commercial and naval power of the day. Colbert discriminated against their trade with high tariffs. He was also determined to match them in naval power. In addition to his other jobs, he became secretary of the navy, and launched a massive programme of building warships, together with a scheme for conscripting sailors. By the time of his death in 1683 he had made Louis XIV's navy the largest and most modern in Europe.

Colbert was also hostile to the "idle" inhabitants

CULTURAL GLORY

The reign of Louis XIV was also the great age of classical French culture. Writers, artists, architects, scholars and musicians all benefited from royal support, promoting and funding their work. The king and his ministers were convinced that their patronage boosted royal prestige and "brought glory to France among foreign nations".

Court theatres proved a receptive audience for the comedies of Molière and the tragedies of Corneille and Racine. Ceremonial religious of monasteries, and sought to discourage entry into religious life. The king, however, was conventionally devout, and saw the church as a pillar of his authority, to be protected so long as it obeyed him. Throughout his early years the clergy had been torn by controversies between power-hungry Jesuits and opponents coalescing around the memory of the austere Flemish theologian Cornelius Jansen.

Many parish clergy in Paris had been Jansenist sympathisers during the Fronde, which left the young king, his suspicions fanned by Jesuit confessors, convinced that Jansenists were congenital rebels. The spiritual headquarters of Jansenism was the female monastery of Port Royal, whose nuns spent years resisting the efforts of crown and papacy to impose an oath (or formulary) on them condemning Jansen's work. It took until 1669 to bring them round to uneasy obedience. But even after this "Peace of the Church", which only

---

occasions, ballets and court festivities were invariably accompanied by the music of such composers as Lully or Charpentier. Bernini made the journey from Italy to Paris to sculpt a memorable bust of the king, and building and landscaping programmes provided plenty of scope for Le Vau, Mansart, Perrault and Lenôtre to design on a grand scale. The interiors of their buildings also needed decoration and adornment with pictures by such artists as Mignard, Largillière or Rigaud, who painted the most famous image of the king. In 1687 the poet Perrault claimed that the age of "Louis the Great" had surpassed the ancient world in cultural attainment. ■

lasted ten years, the tension raised by Jansenism rumbled on, much to the king's irritation.

By then the king was also turning against the Huguenots, a community numbering perhaps 850,000. When his grandfather, Henry IV, had ended the Wars of Religion by becoming a Catholic, his former Protestant co-religionists had secured toleration and a certain protective autonomy in the Edict of Nantes (1598). Their autonomy was lost under Richelieu, but toleration continued, despite the Catholic clergy's persistent clamour for harsher measures.

During the Fronde the Huguenots remained ostentatiously loyal. Turenne, the king's most

ROYAL RESIDENCES

Louvre The king's most ancient palace in the centre of Paris. Louis XIV invited the great Italian architect and sculptor Bernini to design a replacement, but his plans proved too extravagant. Colbert instead commissioned a grand new eastern façade. It is still there, but the king never occupied the Louvre after 1666.

Tuileries A summer residence surrounded by gardens to the west of the Louvre. Colbert set it up as the main seat of the court in 1666, but it was already clear that the king preferred to spend most of his time outside Paris. The palace stood empty for most of the reign and for the subsequent century. It was burnt down in 1871.

Saint-Germain Three hours' ride to the west of Paris, surrounded by forests full of game, it had been a favoured royal palace since medieval times. Louis XIV was born there, and learnt its value as a successful general, was one of them. But the Catholic population, especially in areas of the south and west where Protestants were concentrated, was unremittingly hostile. Nor did the king feel happy ruling a religiously divided realm. His early policy was to maintain the Edict of Nantes but interpret it as narrowly as possible, using every opportunity to push Huguenots towards conversion. When Turenne became a Catholic in 1668 it looked as if this policy was working. Protestants were offered money to convert, although not many succumbed. By 1670, however, the king and his ministers were increasingly distracted from this issue by preparations for war.

---

secure base outside the capital during the Fronde. He spent most of his time at Saint-Germain until moving the court to Versailles in 1682. Seven years later the palace was occupied by the exiled Stuart court of James II. Most of the buildings have now disappeared.

Palais Royal Built next to the Louvre by Cardinal Richelieu for his own use, it was left to the crown in his will. It was the main residence of Anne of Austria and the boy-king during the Regency, until found too vulnerable during the Fronde. In the 1660s it became the seat of the king's brother, Philippe I, duke d'Orléans, and was passed down through his descendants until the 19th century. It was once again the centre of power from 1715 to 1722, during the Regency of Monsieur's son. Nowadays it houses the Council of State.

Fontainebleau To the south of Paris and further out than Saint-Germain, it had been the favourite residence of Francis I, and much embellished by Henry IV. The vast forest surrounding it was ideal for hunting, and Louis XIV moved

How successful were the king's attempts to achieve domination abroad?

Marriage to Maria Teresa of Spain in 1660 proved crucial to the success of Louis XIV's adult reign. The queen was physically un-prepossessing, and once she had fulfilled her first duty of giving the king a male heir, the Grand Dauphin (born in 1661), her husband largely neglected her until her death in 1683. All five of her subsequent children died young. Meanwhile, the lusty young monarch flaunted mistress after mistress. The most successful, from 1667 to 1680, was a duke's daughter,

---

his court there every autumn. Rulers came to hunt regularly until 1814, and the vast palace and its gardens remain largely intact.

Marly The king's private domain built between 1679 and 1686, six miles north of Versailles. It was a retreat from the formal world of Versailles, where he could relax in select company, present by invitation only.

Versailles Louis XIV began to extend what was originally a small hunting lodge to the west of Paris in the 1660s, and undertook a massive rebuilding programme from 1669. It was established as the principal seat of his court in 1682, although building works went on almost until the end of the reign. The overall cost of the palace and its magnificent setting of landscaped gardens was 82 million livres. While it is true that the king disliked Paris and went there less and less frequently, the choice of Versailles owed more to his love of hunting and above all the need for space to house a glittering court than to fearful memories of the capital's turbulent population during the Fronde. ■

Athénaïs de Montespan, who bore the king six children, all of whom he legitimised.

But the queen was more than just a means of prolonging the dynasty. She also provided hope of territorial expansion. In the early years of his reign there was little opportunity for military campaigns, much to the king's regret. But in 1665 the death of his Spanish father-in-law gave him a pretext for making war: the dowry agreed at the Peace of the Pyrenees in return for the queen's renunciation of claims to Spanish inheritance had never been paid. On these grounds her renunciation could be set aside.

The new king in Madrid, Carlos II, was a sickly child from a second marriage. He was not expected to survive long and then, perhaps, the queen of France might hope to inherit his throne. Meanwhile, Brabant law was invoked to claim the Spanish Netherlands. In Brabant, the children of first marriages were not disadvantaged by their parents' remarriage and still inherited property. Thus it was claimed that the territory "devolved" on Maria Teresa (the child of a first marriage), and in 1667 French troops under the command of Turenne seized a number of fortresses in Flanders to secure the queen's "rights". The next year a rehabilitated Condé continued the so-called war of "'Devolution'" by marching unopposed into the Spanish province of Franche Comté, far to the south.

Throughout their long struggle for independence from Spain, the Dutch had been allies of the French, an alliance which persisted even after Dutch independence was finally achieved in 1648. But now they were scared by the French king's ambitions. Rapidly settling their differences with their commercial and naval rivals, the English, who were equally alarmed, they put together a defensive alliance to resist further advances.

Louis XIV felt betrayed, and he never forgot it. Still expecting the Spanish king's early death, he made a secret deal with the Holy Roman Emperor, Leopold I, in which they agreed to divide the Spanish territories between them, with France acquiring all of the Netherlands and Franche Comté. Further military operations now seemed pointless, and in return for the face-saving acquisition of a handful of Flemish fortified towns, notably Lille, France made peace with Spain, and waited.

But Carlos II did not die (and would not for another 32 years), while the Dutch exulted in their success in publicly thwarting Louis XIV's ambitions. The king and his young secretary of war, Le Tellier's son Louvois, were determined to punish them, though it took several years of diplomacy to prepare the next move. Charles II of England was seduced from his Dutch alliance with cash incentives (the Secret Treaty of Dover, 1670) and in 1672 three French armies were launched against the Dutch republic. The attack, violating Spanish territory in Flanders, would, it was hoped, provoke Spain into declaring war, offering the prospect of further legitimate conquests.

The king liked to be present when his generals were expecting victories, and he was present as the southern provinces of the Republic were rapidly overrun, and as the government in Amsterdam collapsed. The untried William, Prince of Orange, was thrust to the head of the Dutch armies in the ancestral office of stadtholder, but they were no match for the invaders and offered to surrender. France's terms were so humiliating, however, that, rather than accept them, the Dutch opened the dykes and turned much of Holland into a lake. The invasion stalled, Amsterdam was saved, and Louis XIV went home.

In 1674 the French withdrew. The war, however, continued, with different objectives. As the king had hoped, Spain was drawn in, and this gave him the excuse to invade Franche Comté once again. But others were now drawn in too, including the Holy Roman Emperor and most of the princes of Germany. The Dutch used their financial resources to hold an anti-French coalition together. Fighting was mostly along the Rhine, and then again in Flanders. After two years, Charles II was forced by the English parliament to make peace. Within two more years the daughter of Charles II's brother James was married to William of Orange – a fateful match for Louis XIV, as it turned out. Peace negotiations were begun in 1676, and peace was finally signed at Nijmegen in 1678.

The Dutch Republic had survived the French

onslaught without substantial loss. It was now led by the intensely francophobe William III. The Spanish Netherlands still eluded Louis XIV's grasp, but their frontier was rationalised, with France acquiring the best-fortified towns. Most significantly, Spain ceded the whole province of Franche Comté, the most important acquisition of the king's adult reign.

It was commemorated by another triumphal arch. Yet a peace that could plausibly be celebrated as glorious left him unsatisfied. Although the Flanders frontier was now secure, between it and newly acquired Franche Comté lay a bewildering palimpsest of territorial confusion, offering Germanic enemies a series of entry points to the heart of the kingdom. The next seven years were spent trying to incorporate these entry points into French territory. Sometimes they were simply occupied, like the fragmented Duchy of Lorraine, coveted by French monarchs since the sixteenth century. Louis XIV bluntly declared that "Lorraine belongs to me", although he never annexed it. The free imperial city of Strasbourg, however, was formally forced to acknowledge the sovereignty of the king of France as he sat outside it in 1681 with an army of 13,000 men.

A whole series of territories was steadily annexed, or notionally "reunited" with the kingdom by the judgement of French courts set up to investigate their legal status. Only one verdict was possible in these cases, but the decisions of

François-Michel le Tellier, Marquis de Louvois

'chambers of reunion' were backed up by troops of the greatest army in Europe. Some were jurisdictionally part of the Holy Roman Empire; others, such as Luxembourg, were dependencies of Spain. The Emperor protested but, beset then by the Turks who almost took Vienna in 1683, had no forces available to reinforce his protests. Carlos II of Spain declared war against France, but found no allies in Europe. In 1684 he and the Emperor agreed to the Truce of Ratisbon under which Louis

XIV would keep his gains provisionally for 20 years.

It was the zenith of the Sun King's power, but it came at a price. Europe had been thoroughly alarmed by his pretensions. Was he aiming, they wondered, at universal monarchy? By this time the 'Most Christian King' had even quarrelled with the Pope over the right to appropriate the revenues of vacant episcopal sees (*régale*). Yet the royal commitment to religious orthodoxy was strengthening: no sooner was the war against the Dutch Protestants over, than pressure was brutally renewed on French ones.

Huguenots were now systematically excluded from public life, their "temples" pulled down, all legal protection eroded. Pressure to convert to Catholicism was reinforced by billeting unruly soldiers on the Huguenot strongholds – the notorious *dragonnades*. Nobody at court spoke up for Protestants, and the king's most recent mistress, Mme de Maintenon, though descended from Huguenots herself, applauded his zeal. Finally, in 1685, the Edict of Nantes was revoked by the Edict of Fontainebleau. Since there were no more Protestants left in the kingdom, it disingenuously declared, toleration had become superfluous. Perhaps the king really believed that the Huguenot problem had been solved. And he had certainly shown the Pope, as well as the Emperor whom he had refused to help against the infidel Turks in 1683, what a sincere son of the Church he was.

Dominant in Europe, the king had at the same time finally restored internal unity to his kingdom – or so it appeared.

What did he achieve in his second reign?*

The *thèse royale* vaunted Louis XIV as the masterful monarch who, with the help of ministers of low birth but high ability, tamed the nobility, silenced the parlements, dazzled the world by building Versailles, and dominated Europe through the strength of his diplomacy and his armies. Much of this picture originated with the king's own propaganda machine, as Peter Burke has shown. Nearly every element in the *thèse royale* has been challenged by the scholarship of the last half-century.

For one thing, the low birth of ministers was only relative: all were nobles rather than the "vile bourgeoisie" denounced by the haughty Duke de Saint-Simon. Their abilities, too, have been called into question. Daniel Dessert, in *Argent, pouvoir et société au Grand Siècle* (1984), sees Colbert as a low intriguer, more interested in promoting the interests of his family and clients than in serving the king. Louvois was scarcely better, once reminding an over-zealous subordinate of his guiding principle that "His Majesty must not be served any better than he wants to be".

* See bibliography for relevant titles

The nobility as a whole, meanwhile – far from being humiliated – found co-operation with the king well rewarded. The few who could afford it flocked to court in pursuit of royal patronage. Guy Rowlands has shown how the expansion of the armies offered unprecedented opportunities for serving profitably, and how all the high commands went to wealthy courtiers. So too did provincial governorships which, as Roger Mettam has demonstrated, were far from eclipsed in influence by intendants.

As for the ostensibly anti-noble policies, such as Colbert's searches for false claims to nobility, these actually *reassured* the nobles who could prove themselves authentic. Much the same point has been made about the parlements by Albert Hamscher, who argues that the crown, rather than undermining them, became deliberately less confrontational and respected their jurisdictional claims. "The key to royal control," argues Hamscher, "lay in management rather than innovation, in supervision rather than in reorganisation." When in 1673 the king forbade remonstrances until after edicts were registered, the measure was largely symbolic: it was already six years since the parlement of Paris had made any remonstrances at all.

Such revisionism has not gone uncontested. John J. Hurt has claimed in the case of the parlements that the crown *did* behave with all the haughty brutality noted by adherents of the *thèse royale*: "Absolute government, whatever ornate compromises decorated its multiple facades, rested on an authoritarian foundation." The most resolute revisionists, however, such as Nicholas Henshall(see bibliography), argue that the very idea of absolutism is a myth, and that the term should be abandoned entirely.

There has been less disagreement about Louis XIV's diplomatic and military adventures during the Second Reign. Most historians have seen him as aggressively ambitious. An influential exception is Ragnhild Hatton, who argues that France was beset by devious rivals seeking ways to subvert the settlement of the Peace of Westphalia, and that the king's "foreign policy reactions may be labelled defensive in intent, even when war ensued". Hatton points out how often war was first declared by the Emperor or the king of Spain, but even she finds it hard to justify the reunions, although explaining clearly enough why they were undertaken. And, as Paul Sonnino has shown, Louis XIV was determined - and had been determined for several years before 1672 -, to punish the Dutch for thwarting his earlier designs on the southern Netherlands. Colbert, anxious as ever to destroy Dutch commercial competition, still thought it too soon to try, but was forced to recognise that by 1672 it was "the only game in town".

TEN FACTS ABOUT LOUIS XIV

1.
The American state of Louisiana is named after Louis XIV. It was under French control between 1682 to 1763 and again from 1800 to 1803 and was known as La Louisiane (Land of Louis).

2.
His gradual adoption from the 1650s of wigs to disguise his thinning hair set a Europe-wide fashion for male wigs which lasted until the French Revolution. He is said to have ended up owning more than 1,000 wigs.

3.
It is sometimes claimed that Louis only had three baths in his life. In fact, he bathed regularly in a large Turkish bath, disinfected his skin with spirits or alcohol and changed his clothes several times a day.

4.
Red heels were worn by Louis XIV's courtiers from 1662, after the king adopted the fashion from his brother.

5.
He never gave an instant decision, always responding "I'll see".

6.
He was married twice, although firm documentary evidence of his marriage to Mme. de Maintenon has never been found. He had three sons and three daughters by Queen Maria Teresa, but all died in infancy except Louis the Grand Dauphin, who still predeceased his father by four years. He also had at least five mistresses, who gave him at least ten illegitimate children.

7.
He was 5 feet 5 inches tall, but looked taller in his wig and heels.

8.
His huge appetite was served by a special department called "The King's Mouth", but he drank little, and his wine was always watered.

9.
Louis XIV commissioned more than 300 portraits of himself, many of which survive today.

10.
When he died, the king's body was taken at night to lie among his ancestors at Saint-Denis, but not in secret as has often been claimed. More than a thousand mourners accompanied his coffin.

THE THIRD REIGN, 1680s-1715: the limits of ambition

Why did things go wrong?

The 1680s brought Louis XIV's power to a triumphant peak. His territorial conquests reached their maximum extent. His court moved permanently to the magnificent new palace at Versailles. Unprecedented royal authority was established over the church; and (officially at least) after a century and a half of tolerating Protestant dissent, religious uniformity was restored to the kingdom.

But the glory days were almost over. The great ministers who had helped to mould them were dying off: Colbert in 1683, Le Tellier in 1685. Colbert's son Seignelay, succeeding him as navy minister, only lasted until 1690. Even Louvois, Le Tellier's influential son, died in 1691. In 1683 the queen died and the king contracted a secret morganatic marriage to his last mistress, Françoise de Maintenon.* She would be a devout and constant companion for the rest of his life, consoling him through the tribulations to come.

---

* A morganatic marriage is one between people of unequal status, which prevents the higher-ranking husband's titles and possessions passing on to the lower-ranking wife, or to any children born to them.

Françoise de Maintenon, Louis XIV's second wife

Some of these were physical. He had attacks of gout. He lost most of his teeth, and parts of his jaw. In 1686-7 an anal fistula developed, only cured by painful surgery. After this he no longer danced much, and hunted far less often. From 1693 he ceased to accompany his troops on campaign. His appetites whether at table or, (according to Mme de Maintenon,) in bed were scarcely diminished, nor his methodical commitment to everyday business. But that business would never again be as straightforward as in the days of his young manhood.

When in 1683 he refused help to the Emperor Leopold against the Turks, Louis XIV's hope was that imperial forces would collapse, leaving the French army, the largest and best in Europe, as the only possible saviour of Christendom. He even seems to have dreamed of succeeding Leopold as Holy Roman Emperor. The relief of Vienna by the Emperor's Polish and German allies destroyed this dream. The Habsburgs were reinvigorated, chasing the Turks south, but they always remembered French indifference to their earlier plight.

Nor did the decision to revoke the Edict of Nantes have the desired effect. He had hoped it would restore his damaged religious reputation. But the Pope was unimpressed. He rightly thought that it would intensify the persecution of Catholics in Protestant states. It did more damage than that. Persecution of the Huguenots drove perhaps 200,000 of them into exile, carrying tales of Catholic cruelties, and taking with them industrial and commercial skills to benefit France's economic competitors in England, Holland, and north Germany. Huguenot writers in exile trumpeted the French king's tyranny. In Germany the Elector of Brandenburg, opening his frontiers to a stream of refugee Calvinist co-religionists, broke a six-year alliance with France to join the League of Augsburg, a pact to defend the Holy Roman Empire against French ambitions.

And across the Channel, the revocation coincided with the accession of James II, who was determined to restore his three kingdoms to his own Catholic faith. The revocation was a warning to his apprehensive Anglican and Presbyterian subjects of what might await them if he succeeded. It was not even as if persecution worked within Louis XIV's own kingdom. Protestantism had not been stamped out, and forced "conversions" continued throughout the 1690s. In Languedoc, the crackdown on Protestants provoked an apocalyptic fanaticism in the remote communities of the Cévennes mountains which culminated in 1702 in the rebellion of the Camisards, the greatest internal revolt which the mature king ever had to face. For two years the rebels tied down more than 10,000 troops. Sporadic resistance flickered on

GALLICANISM

While accepting the spiritual authority of the pope, the French church had a long tradition of jurisdictional independence. Under the Concordat of Bologna (1516) the king appointed all bishops, the Pope merely conferring their spiritual powers. The autonomy of the French church was periodically asserted in the assembly of the clergy, meeting every five years. It was also defended by the parlements, who held that papal bulls and pronouncements were only valid in France if registered in the king's courts.

Louis XIV's quarrel with the Pope over the crown's right to the revenues of vacant episcopal sees led to a proclamation – by the assembly of the clergy – of the four "Gallican articles" of 1682. Drafted by Bishop Bossuet of Meaux, these declared that royal authority was superior to the pope's within the kingdom – that papal powers were only spiritual, and were subject to the consent of the church as a whole. The articles were suspended when the quarrel with the Pope was patched up, but they were revived by Napoleon over a century later. ■

until 1709. There is no doubt that the king's persecution of his Protestant subjects was widely approved throughout his overwhelmingly Catholic realm, but it had effects both at home and abroad which made it the greatest mistake of his reign.

It was not the only religious issue to disturb his later years. His quarrel with the Pope, inaugurated over regalian rights in 1673, and widened by the adoption of the Gallican articles, went on until 1693. During that time successive pontiffs refused to confer spiritual powers on new French bishops, and at one point in 1688 the king was even secretly excommunicated. It took renewed Europe-wide warfare to persuade Innocent XII to accept a mutual agreement to drop the quarrels. He and his successor, Clement XI, proved more willing to co-operate with royal religious policies, but the co-operation caused fresh problems.

Irritated by continuing polemics over Jansenism after the Peace of the Church, in 1679 the king renewed measures against what he called "those endless Port-Royal people". The convent was forbidden to admit new entrants, and its main intellectual defenders went into exile. But sniping continued among theologians, and as the century ended a new generation resurrected issues going back beyond the Peace of the Church. Evidence emerged in 1703 of a Europe-wide network of clandestine Jansenist correspondence, and when two years later a fresh papal bull at royal request renewed fifty-year-old sanctions against Jansenist doctrines, the ageing nuns of Port Royal once more defied them. They were expelled from their convent, and the site was subsequently levelled.

To stamp out Jansenism once and for all, the king and a stern new Jesuit confessor asked the Pope for a definitive and comprehensive condemnation. Accordingly, in 1713 Clement XI promulgated the bull *Unigenitus*, which denounced as seditious and heretical 101 propositions from a popular work by Pasquier Quesnel, a leading Jansenist exile. Contrary to royal expectations, there was uproar. The bull embodied papal pretensions never before accepted in France. Even the king, jurists argued, had no right to allow it. Magistrates, bishops, divines, and hundreds of pamphleteers openly denounced it. The king was astounded and outraged. Never since the Fronde had royal authority been so openly defied. He was preparing to impose *Unigenitus* by force when death claimed him. The issue would poison public life in the kingdom for decades to come.

Louis XIV largely brought the religious problems of his later reign upon himself. Other difficulties, however, were completely beyond his control. Adverse weather dogged his time on the throne, which coincided with the "little ice age" of the 17th century. The Dutch War of the 1670s was fought amid violent climatic fluctuations. It was torrential rain in the summer of 1672 which made the opening of the dykes so effective a defence; and the internal revolts of 1675 came in a "year without a summer", when crops failed and heavy war taxes became unaffordable.

The 1680s brought some respite; but in 1693, in time of war again, famine struck, followed by widespread lethal epidemics on a scale not seen for half a century. Then came a bitter winter, and, by the time conditions improved late in 1694, the kingdom's population had fallen by 1.7 million.

The new century began with several benign years, but they came to a brutal end with the "Great Winter" of 1709, when temperatures fell to arctic levels for three months. It was impossible to grow a proper harvest. Trees were devastated, animals froze. Bread prices soared, and there were widespread riots. The death toll was only a third of that in the crisis of 1693-4, but, coming at the nadir of France's military fortunes in the Spanish Succession War, the impact of the Great Winter was remembered for far longer.

Shivering in glacial Versailles, the king shared some of the distress of his subjects. Soon afterwards he was struck by an improbable series of personal and dynastic calamities. In April 1711 his only legitimate son, Louis the Grand Dauphin, died of smallpox. Two years later the next in line, the Duke de Bourgogne, his wife, and their elder son were carried away in a measles epidemic. Then Bourgogne's brother was killed in a riding accident. The sole surviving legitimate male descendant of the great king by 1714 was Bourgogne's second son, the two-year-old Anjou – apart from Philip V of Spain, who, at the insistence of the other powers of Europe, had renounced his claim to the French throne.

Faced with the possible sudden extinction of his line, the king in desperation conferred rights of succession on his two legitimised sons by Mme de Montespan: the Duke du Maine and the Count de Toulouse. Many thought this an even greater flouting of the fundamental laws of the kingdom than the imposition of *Unigenitus*. If monarchs could alter the very law of succession by which they reigned, then there was no law but their own caprice. None dared say this openly while the king lived, but this step too far did not long survive him. During the last few years of his life, however, it seems clear that the seemingly unchallengeable authority which he had built up so confidently over more than half a century was beginning to crumble.

How did French expansion lose momentum?

Louis XIV never intended that the war he launched in 1688 should last so long or cost so much. His aim was simple, and ostensibly defensive: to force the Emperor and the German states of the League of Augsburg to give permanent recognition to French territorial gains made between 1679 and the Truce of Ratisbon five years later. In 1687 they refused. The French were increasingly afraid, as the Turks were driven south across the Balkans, that the

Emperor would soon be able to redeploy seasoned armies in Germany to reinforce his refusal.

Using the pretext of a disputed election to the princely archbishopric of Cologne, a pre-emptive strike into the Rhineland was planned, further consolidating the kingdom's new frontier by taking the strategic fortress of Philippsburg. The king became aware, as he marshalled his forces, that his sworn enemy William III had been invited by Anglican opponents of James II to save them from their Catholic ruler.

The stadholder was preparing an army to cross the Channel. A French foray into the Netherlands, Louis XIV knew, could have prevented the prince's departure, but he took no action: even if William III reached England unopposed, he concluded, the most likely outcome would be another civil war in Britain, leaving the stadholder marooned and the Dutch Republic leaderless. Instead the French pressed on with the invasion of the Rhineland, and, after a six-week siege, Philippsburg surrendered.

A week later, William III landed in England, unopposed either by James II's navy or, later, by his army. There was no civil war. James II fled to France, and, by the spring of 1689 the stadholder was installed with his wife Mary on the British thrones. Meanwhile, Louis XIV had extended his campaign to the entire Rhineland. His tactic was to devastate the entire region, stripping it of natural resources which might prove useful to an enemy and thus ensuring that it would pose no threat to France.

Portrait of Louis XIV by Hyacinthe Rigaud (1701)

"Remove from your mind," Louvois told French commanders, "that you need spare the Germans anything out of friendship or moderation. Plenty of cannon and fortresses in their country will subdue them better than anything else." This might have seemed to make military sense, but its effect on public opinion in Germany and beyond was disastrous. In the course of 1689 all the major German princes united behind the Emperor to oppose the French, and William III brought the maritime power of both the Dutch and English into the coalition. Spain also joined, reopening a front in the southern Netherlands. Louis XIV's miscalculations had brought together the whole of Europe against him.

Much of his power depended upon the resources of his kingdom, the most populous in Europe, from which he was able to recruit and pay for the largest armed forces. French armies had already reached unprecedented size in the wars between 1635 and 1659. Upon his assumption of personal authority the king could rely on a standing army of around 50,000. For the War of Devolution it almost doubled, and the Dutch War of 1672 was undertaken with planned forces of 150,000. This had risen to 250,000 by the time it ended. The unexpected resistance of most of the other European powers to French demands in the war from 1688 onwards, with combined forces now outnumbering the king's (on paper at least), brought a further swelling of his own to around 340,000. It would be another century before such numbers were seen again.

This military expansion had been matched by the creation of an equally formidable navy. Essentially Colbert's personal project, it was protected after his death by his son Seignelay. By the end of the Dutch War France already had the largest battle fleet in Europe, although it was now provoking a naval arms race with the English and Dutch. Fabulously expensive and not easy to man, this fleet ruthlessly bombarded undefended Genoa in 1684, but was not seriously tested until 1689, when it successfully carried James II and a supporting French force to Ireland. The next year it worsted the combined English and Dutch fleets at Beachy Head. But in 1692, at La Hogue, the allies inflicted a heavy defeat on a French fleet which had been preparing to invade England in an ill-planned attempt to restore James II to the throne. Seignelay, dying in 1690, could no longer defend big-fleet operations before his sceptical master, who had only ever seen a warship once. French efforts at sea were now increasingly diverted to a cheaper but more effective war on trade, conducted mainly by privateers.

With occasional cracks, the anti-French coalition held together for six years. They fought the French in Ireland, Flanders, northern Italy and Catalonia, as well as in Germany. France's only friends were the Turks, who periodically rolled back Austrian forces in the Balkans. And whereas James II and his French auxiliaries were defeated by William III at the Boyne in Ireland in 1690, the French won most of the battles and sieges on the continent.

Yet by 1696 it had long been clear that the conflict had reached stalemate. The allies had fought Louis XIV to a standstill. The coalition began to break up, as Victor Amadeus of Savoy-Piedmont switched sides. Rumours of the king of Spain's deteriorating health, led to new fears that the long-shelved issue of the Spanish succession might re-ignite. Attempts to find some sort of resolution to the conflict had been going on since 1693 and now these efforts suddenly reached a rapid resolution – in the Peace of Ryswick of 1697.

Announcing the terms with characteristic loftiness, Louis XIV declared: "I sacrificed the advantages that I gained in the war... to public tranquillity." And certainly, for the first time in his reign, he gave up territory, including Luxembourg, some of the lesser reunions, Philippsburg where the war began, and his long-standing claim to Lorraine. Of what he had held at the Truce of Ratisbon not much more than Strasbourg remained in his hands. He recognised the right of his inveterate enemy, William III, to the British thrones, though insisting on treating James II, now his exiled guest in France, as a king. He allowed the Dutch to garrison a number of barrier fortresses in the southern Netherlands. He made few concessions to the Emperor, but could do little but watch as, over the next two years, imperial forces forced the Turks into the humiliating Peace of Carlowitz (1699). France had not been defeated; but it was now clear that the days when Louis XIV could overawe and intimidate his neighbours were over.

How expensive were these military adventures?

The effort of achieving such a mediocre result had been enormous, especially against the background of severe economic difficulties at the height of hostilities in 1693-4. The amount spent on military infrastructure had been colossal. There were vast new naval dockyards at Brest, Rochefort and Toulon. And the king's long-term strategy on land had been to establish what he called a "field of fire" (*pré carré*), a coherent frontier of heavily fortified strong-points, designed by the great military engineer Vauban, which any invading army would be forced to besiege before advancing into the kingdom. Building the increasingly elaborate defences of such fortresses absorbed huge resources. Once established, they also needed credible garrisons and supplies to withstand sieges. And armed forces of a size never seen before had to be equipped and fed – even when famine and disease were ravaging the kingdom.

The organisational achievements of Louvois, however, were far more impressive than his strategic and tactical instincts. Military recruitment was actually boosted by famine, since feeding the army was the first claim on meagre harvests. Swollen forces also gave employment to glory-hunting noblemen as officers, who were often contracted by the crown to raise their own units. Armies on campaign ruthlessly extracted the wealth of occupied enemy territories, but their yield inevitably fluctuated with the fortunes of war.

Within the kingdom, meanwhile, all the "extraordinary" money-making expedients so familiar in wartime since 1635 were reactivated – sales or "confirmations" of privileges; the creation of new venal offices and the blackmail of their holders; the extension of venality to new provinces like Franche Comté; innumerable schemes suggested by and contracted out to *traitants*. All were designed to make office-holders bear part of the cost of the war. To do this they had to borrow, in effect giving the crown access to credit it could not obtain by other means.

But even the previously tax-exempt elites, (from whom the office-holders had to borrow) were themselves forced to make sacrifices. In 1695 a poll-tax, the *capitation*, was introduced, payable on a sliding scale by all the king's subjects, including the nobility. (The only exception was the clergy.) For the first time, then, nobles were subjected to direct taxation, modest though it was. The capitation was abandoned two years later, when the war ended, along with many other extraordinary measures. But not for long. The return of peace was to prove very short-lived.

Why another war?

Never, since 1665, had the Spanish succession been far from Louis XIV's mind. Every rumoured sickness of the childless king of Spain triggered a diplomatic alert. Both Louis XIV and the Emperor Leopold were the sons and husbands of Spanish infantas. These princesses had all, on marriage, renounced their rights in the succession to the Spanish throne for themselves and their heirs, but the validity of their renunciations was never beyond dispute. Invoking the claims of their respective wives, the king and the Emperor had agreed in 1668 to divide the Spanish inheritance between them if, as expected, Carlos II died without issue. But this agreement lapsed when the two monarchs went to war in the 1670s, and on joining the anti-French coalition a decade later the Spanish king promised that the Emperor's heirs should succeed him as rulers of an undivided inheritance.

Louis XIV, whose own heirs had comparable claims, was never likely to accept this. He had spent his whole adult life laying claim to Spanish territories; he still thought that his family deserved a share of them. But after nine years of debilitating warfare he shrank from further fighting to secure it. Consulting neither Vienna nor Madrid, he made an agreement with William III in 1698 to avoid another war by recognising the Emperor Leopold's Bavarian grandson as heir to all of the Spanish empire except the Italian territories, which would be divided between Austria and France. But this agreement lapsed the next year when the grandson died. The two rulers then negotiated a second partition treaty under which Leopold's second son by a second marriage – the Archduke Charles – would inherit the entire Spanish Empire except the Italian territories.

Again, the Austrians were not consulted, although Italy was what they coveted most; and above all the agreement ignored Spanish opinion which was overwhelmingly against any division of the worldwide empire. Carlos II shared this view, and shortly before he died in 1700 he made a will which stipulated that the undivided Spanish inheritance should go to the claimant he thought most likely to keep it together: Louis XIV's grandson, the Duke d'Anjou. Should his bequest be refused, it would be offered to the Archduke Charles.

Louis XIV was now faced with the greatest dilemma of his reign. To accept the will meant war – certainly against the Emperor, newly strengthened by his victorious peace with the Turks; and possibly against William III as a consequence of reneging on the second partition treaty. But to refuse the bequest to his grandson was to concede international hegemony to the House of Austria.

To the surprise of the Spanish ambassador, the king hesitated. But as usual at important moments, he was taking advice. And in the end he accepted the will, though it was several days before he presented his grandson to the court as Philip V of Spain. The ecstatic ambassador declared that the Pyrenees were no more, but the will had explicitly stated that France and Spain should never be united, and Louis XIV accepted this. He hoped his acceptance would reassure the maritime powers enough to prevent them joining the Emperor in a new anti-French coalition.

Initially it did so. The British and the Dutch offered no support when the Emperor sent troops into Spanish Lombardy in the name of "Carlos III" (the Archduke Charles). But then a series of provocative French blunders changed their attitude. The king declared that the new Spanish king could not forfeit his rights, however seemingly remote, in the French line of succession. He sent "auxiliary" troops into the Spanish Netherlands, expelling Dutch garrisons from their newly-conceded barrier fortresses. He persuaded Spain to make the supply of slaves to its American empire (*asiento*) a French monopoly. And when the exiled James II died, he recognised his son as the legitimate British monarch – a flagrant breach of the peace of Ryswick, and an insult to William III. William III himself died a few months later, to be succeeded by James's daughter Anne, but not before a new alliance had been struck between the British, the Dutch and the Emperor. Its primary object was to put the Archduke Charles on the throne of Spain.

So began Louis XIV's last great war. For the most part it was disastrous. Although this time France never lacked allies, it was fought on as many fronts as before. Spain, now for the first time in generations a French ally, was torn by civil war, with imperial and French troops supporting the conflicting sides. The generals of Louis XIV's glory days – Turenne, Condé, Luxembourg – were unmatched by any of the new generation apart from Villars. The allied side, in contrast, instead of the dogged but untalented William III, could call upon the military brilliance of Prince Eugene of Savoy (who had once been refused service in the French army by Louis XIV) and the Duke of Marlborough. The latter inflicted bloody defeats on the French at Blenheim (1704) and Ramillies (1706), while Eugene drove most of the French out of northern Italy. To peace feelers sent out by the shaken French, the allied response was, "no peace without Spain". This Louis XIV could not accept, but by 1708 he had suffered further catastrophic losses. His armies were defeated by Marlborough again at Oudenarde, and Lille, the proudest acquisition of his early reign and Vauban's most vaunted fortified citadel, was lost. The fortress frontier had been breached, and the way to Paris stood open.

These losses coincided with the "Great Winter" of 1709, and drove France to the brink of surrender. The financial effort of renewing such wide-ranging hostilities so soon after the previous draining conflict had already taken the kingdom to the brink of bankruptcy. As soon as fighting resumed all measures to pay down the debts of the previous war had been suspended. The *capitation* tax was re-imposed. New privileges were sold, fresh forced loans were extracted from holders of venal offices, and hosts of predatory new ones were created. *Traitants* and their schemes flourished as never before, although by 1708 employing such private intermediaries was beginning to cost more than they were contributing. There was also periodic manipulation or reminting of the currency, with all its destabilising economic consequences. Increasing shortages of cash now led to experiments with paper money (*billets de monnaie* or mint bills), but far too much of this was issued and it plummeted in value.

By 1708 all forms of credit were beginning to run out. Chamillart, in charge of the finances since 1699, was replaced by Colbert's nephew, Desmaretz. The king himself, reduced to melting down his gold plate, was in despair. In contrast to his brusque ultimatum to Colbert decades earlier (above, p.43), he told his new minister

> that he knew perfectly the state of his finances, that he was not asking the impossible; that if I succeeded, I would render him a great service for which he would be very grateful; if the upshot was not happy, he would not blame me for events.

And France only survived his first year in office, Desmaretz later recalled, by "a kind of miracle".

Why did the king back down?

The king asked the allies for peace terms. They demanded that he should accept the Archduke as king of Spain, surrender key fortresses and strongpoints including Strasbourg, and allow the Dutch to re-garrison their barrier. All this he appeared ready to accept. But he was also required, if Philip V should refuse to leave Spain, to send troops to drive his own grandson out, and at this he baulked. The dishonour was too much, and he resolved to fight on.

By now there was widespread rioting as the army sucked scarce supplies from the famine-stricken kingdom. There were also ominous military mutinies. For the first time in his reign, the king issued a direct appeal to his subjects:

> I wish my people to know ... that they would be enjoying peace had it depended on my will alone to bring them a benefit that they rightly desire but which must be gained by new efforts, since the conditions which I would have offered are useless for the reestablishment of public tranquillity.

This appeal stirred the nobility, at least; but in any case the tide began to turn soon afterwards. Malplaquet in 1709 was indeed another allied victory, but a Pyrrhic one, a slaughter in which the allies lost twice as many men as the French. The next year, with the allies bogged down in Flanders

Portrait of Claude Louis Hector de Villars (1653-1734)

sieges, Philip V's armies – with French support – drove the Austrians back into Catalonia. Then, in the spring of 1711, the Emperor Joseph, who had succeeded his father Leopold in 1705, died with no male heir. The Archduke Charles now became Emperor Charles VI; but Austria's maritime allies, Britain and the Netherlands, had no more wish to see Spain united with Austria than with France. The British had already opened secret peace negotiations in 1710, and as 1712 dawned Marlborough was dismissed. Weakened by British withdrawal, Eugene's imperial and Dutch army was routed at Denain – and this brought the remaining allies to the negotiating table.

The peace-making process was protracted. The last fighting (in Spain) was only resolved three months before Louis XIV died. Considering how close he had come to total defeat, the king did well from the final effort of 1709-12. Yet more money had been raised from squeezing office-holders, borrowing at ruinous rates, and introducing a new direct tax without privileged exemptions, the tenth (*dixième*), convincing the allies that France was not as close to exhaustion as they had thought. Under agreements signed at Utrecht (1713) and Rastatt (1714), Philip V kept the throne of Spain and most of its empire for the Bourbons – although with the firm assurance (vital as so many of Louis XIV's heirs died off) that the two kingdoms should never be united. France lost none of its territorial gains in Europe, and even won a few further enclaves (including William III's former principality of Orange), although the king's lifelong claim to Lorraine remained unfulfilled. Meanwhile, the Dutch kept their barrier fortresses, and the Emperor gained the southern Netherlands and northern Italy. France recognised the Protestant succession in the British Isles, and her loss to Britain of most overseas outposts and the Spanish *asiento*.

It was a peace of exhaustion on all sides; but the conflict had cost France far more than her opponents. Louis XIV had achieved his primary war aim, but only by almost bankrupting his kingdom. The process of financial recovery promised to be almost as painful as the war effort itself. Coming at a moment of dynastic crisis and internal discontent not seen for 40 years, it no doubt played its part in eroding the king's legendary stamina, which finally deserted him on 1st September 1715.

How have historians judged the third reign?*

Until quite recently, the third reign received far less attention from historians than the earlier phases of Louis XIV's rule. It lacked the brilliant achievements of the first decades of his personal government, and it lacked, too, the heroic collaborators who helped him bring them about. The king was more dogged, devout, and indeed downright dull than in his younger days. Magnificent though it was, Versailles, now the main seat of government, was a mournful place for much of his third reign.

The period was not without its triumphs, but they were only achieved after long and arduous efforts. Bureaucracy, argued Georges Pagès in *La Monarchie d'Ancien Régime en France* (1928), had stifled creativity and royal freedom of action. "It is hard to imagine Louis XIV," he wrote, "living, as

---

* See bibliography for relevant titles

formerly Louis XIII and Richelieu, or Mazarin had done, forever improvising, and through endless expedients." Yet this is precisely the picture of how he did live that has emerged from more recent research.

Wars intended to be swift and decisive, as in 1672 or 1689, or conflicts that might have been limited with more caution on the king's part, as in 1702, became prolonged struggles that could only be financed by well-tried expedients and, in the case of the Spanish Succession, an additional range of desperate new experiments that brought the monarchy to the verge of bankruptcy. Recoinages (i.e. creating new coins) and issuing far too much paper money steadily sapped the crown's credit, and the bankers and financiers on whom it relied to keep funds flowing charged ever more exorbitant premiums for their services. "Only the exit of Great Britain from the war in the early summer of 1712," writes Guy Rowlands in *The Financial Decline of a Great Power*, allowed France "to avoid logistical collapse and financial shutdown . . . The country was heading over a cliff.".

Yet, in contrast to the time of the cardinals, and even to the earlier years of personal rule, there were few popular rebellions against the relentless fiscal pressure. The only substantial revolt of these later years, the Camisard uprising, was religious in inspiration, and Gregory Monahan, concludes that it was little more than a minor distraction from the European war. The king and his ministers, argues

Monahan, "simply did not care very much about the rebellion and war in Languedoc".

Nevertheless, the king's anti-Protestant crusade culminating in the revocation of the Edict of Nantes, was a terrible miscalculation. Few historians have defended it, although some with Catholic sympathies have come close. All have recognised the economic benefits which Huguenot refugees took to the Protestant countries where they settled. It was once believed that the French economy suffered commensurate losses. Most, however, now accept the conclusions of Warren C. Scoville that the bulk of the damage suffered by the French economy in the generation after the revocation is attributable not to the loss of Huguenot wealth and skills, but to war, disease, famine, and economic mismanagement.

A further contrast with earlier times was that intense fiscal pressure on the elites led to no repetition of the Fronde. Lionel Rothkrug, in *Opposition to Louis XIV. The political and social origins of the French Enlightenment* (1965), argues that there was in fact a current of opposition, with ministers during these years increasingly beset by doubt and uncertainty, while "a powerful reform movement developed both within and without the administration". More recent historians, however, are not convinced. There was indeed talk of reform, which originated at the royal court, but talk of reform is not the same as resistance.

Meanwhile, the tacit bargain struck between the

monarchy and social elites after the Fronde continued to hold. Most of the old king's subjects could not remember more disobedient times, and had grown up amid constant reminders of how insecure they had been. Although nobles were subjected to direct taxes for the first time in the Third Reign, they were prepared to believe assurances that these were temporary wartime measures. Otherwise privileges positively proliferated, as the socially ambitious queued up to buy them. Why impose unpopular taxes, when subjects would willingly hand over the same money to buy tokens of social distinction? This calculation had served the monarchy well since the 16th century, and Louis XIV and his ministers saw no reason to abandon it.

Legacies, 1715-1815

In what state did Louis XIV leave his kingdom?

The first act of Louis XIV's reign had been the quashing of his father's will in the Parlement of Paris. Did he wonder whether the same thing would happen to his own will? It seems not. He knew there must be a regency, since his only surviving direct heir was an infant, and an orphan. With some trepidation, he designated his dissolute nephew

Philippe, Duke d'Orléans, son of his brother Monsieur (d.1701), as regent. But he circumscribed the regent's power by subjecting it to a council comprising ministers, generals, and not least his two legitimised sons Maine and Toulouse.

The very day after he died – at the regent's request – the will was quashed in the parlement. Like Anne of Austria in 1643, Orléans was accorded full powers until the new King's majority. And in return the parlement was given the right, lost in 1673, to remonstrate against new laws before and not after registering them. Meanwhile, the royal child was whisked away from the scene of death at Versailles. For the next seven years neither he nor the regent's court would reside in the great palace that Louis XIV had created. Paris, which the king only visited eight times since the the court moved to Versailles was once more the undisputed capital of the kingdom.

Forces stifled over half a century now suddenly burst out to challenge monarchical authority. It is true that stirrings of discontent had never been entirely eliminated. French Protestantism had survived Louis XIV's attacks, and had given a focus to criticisms, published abroad, of the excesses of absolute monarchy. And while the heir presumptive Bourgogne was alive, he was seen as a source of hope to a circle of discontented courtiers who believed he might prove a different sort of king from his grandfather.

The intellectual inspiration for these courtiers

was Fénelon, tutor to the young Bourgogne and later Archbishop of Cambrai. They dreamt of a regime which would put more emphasis on public Christian morality, take steps to curb worldly commercialism favoured ever since Colbert, restore the authority of the higher nobility, and seek international peace. But Fénelon became tainted by involvement with a mystical devotional cult called Quietism, condemned by the Pope, and spent his last 18 years exiled in his diocese. In any case, Bourgogne died before inheriting the throne. And so, apart from the Camisard rebellion, and transient mutinous rumblings during the crisis of 1708-9, the most overt internal resistance to Louis XIV after 1675 came only in the last two years of his reign, with the loud and quite unexpected opposition to the bull *Unigenitus*.

This proved one of the king's most enduring and toxic legacies. His obsession with stamping out the last vestiges of Jansenism (one policy which Fénelon had entirely supported) actually rekindled controversies which were almost extinct. Preparations to force acceptance of the bull on to the church and the parlement were abandoned as soon as he died. The Pope, however, felt unable to backtrack, and the regent's efforts to still controversy by ignoring it proved fruitless. Thousands of clergy backed four bishops in 1717 when they appealed to a future general council of the church against the bull and the papal rights it implicitly claimed.

Philippe, Duke d'Orléans, saluting his army on the battlefield

Eventually, in 1731, the parlement was forced to register *Unigenitus* as a law of church and state; but it was not until Jansenism's most resolute and persistent enemies, the Jesuits, were dissolved in the 1760s and 70s that it began to lose its ability to disrupt French public life. Born in the same year as Louis XIV (when Jansen's notorious *Augustinus* was first published), Jansenism had dogged his entire reign. Thanks to *Unigenitus*, it did the same for that of his successor.

In his attempt to reshape the government, the regent not only abandoned Versailles, but made sincere efforts to implement some of the ideas of the Bourgogne circle. In deference to the outrage felt by peers and princes at the old king's tampering with the law of succession, the quashing of his will was followed two years later by the removal of Maine and Toulouse from the legitimate line, along with their status as princes of the blood. It was the climax of a movement that had seen the handful of ministers through which Louis XIV had ruled supplanted by councils dominated by the sort of grandees excluded from executive power ever since 1661.

This council-based system of government, the so-called *Polysynodie,* was not a success. Government business was immobilised by endless disputes among touchy aristocrats about procedure and precedence. In 1718 the frustrated regent dissolved most of the new councils and restored ministerial authority to bureaucrats trained in administration. From then on, until the French Revolution, kings would operate central government much as Louis XIV had. Most minsters continued to be recruited, as before, from the Parisian nobility of the robe, and often the same families. Rising to prominence under Louis XIV, for example, the d'Argensons provided ministers until 1757, the Phélypeaux until 1781. Louis XV even began his majority, like his great grandfather, under the tutelage of a cardinal first minister, Fleury. Fleury's longevity meant that the king did not govern on his own until he was 33. The court, however, moved back to Versailles in 1722, even before the regency ended. The young king, like his great ancestor, found it more convenient for the hunting.

The greatest contrast between the two reigns was in the role of the parlements. Like Anne of Austria, Orléans was beholden to the Parisian court for removing the constraints which the dying king had hoped to place on his power. With its right of remonstrance fully restored, as before the Fronde, the Paris parlement exploited the ambiguous status of a regency to intervene in high policy. A prolonged confrontation between the regent and the magistrates involving religion and finance between 1718 and 1720 led (after half a century of disuse) to *lits de justice* and provincial exile for the parlement. Matters were quickly resolved: but after the regency ended the parlement clung to its role as the watchdog of legality. *Lits de justice* and punitive exiles became regular features of public life.

From the mid-century provincial parlements began to follow the Parisian example, obstructing the work of intendants. Periodically Louis XV felt obliged to reassert full royal authority: although the prohibition on remonstrances before registration was never reimposed, in the last years of his reign draconian reforms reduced the parlements to quiescence. But these reforms were widely seen as despotic, and their unpopularity persuaded Louis XVI on his accession to revoke them. The parlements went on in the 1780s to play a key part in mobilising the public discontent which brought down France's absolute monarchy.

Much of the strength of the parlements derived from the venal tenure of their magistrates. In the 1660s Colbert had dreamed of buying out venality, but the borrowing needs of the wars from 1672 onwards made it too useful to do without. Only in the 1790s would revolutionaries find a way to liquidate this massive long-term debt. But the total debt bequeathed by over a generation of almost continuous warfare far exceeded the capital represented by offices alone. Debt was almost impossible to estimate precisely, but it certainly ran to well over two billion livres. Annual outgoings were far greater than revenues, and income was anticipated several years in advance.

Retrenchment began as soon as peace was signed, while Louis XIV still lived, but gathered pace enormously when he died. As in 1661, a chamber of justice arraigned and fined the most notorious *traitants*. But after the abandonment of *Polysynodie* far more drastic steps were taken. The regent entrusted the finances to a Scottish adventurer, John Law, whose "system" was to set up a state-sponsored bank similar to those which had enabled the Dutch and the English to bear the cost of war borrowing. Confidence in its activities would be sustained by the profits of a colonial trading company which – its shares having been massively oversubscribed by optimistic investors – was progressively allowed to take over much of the state's financial apparatus, and convert royal debts into stock. Eventually the company absorbed the bank and underwrote the paper money it had issued.

But the transatlantic commercial prospects underpinning the whole system were far too meagre to sustain speculative confidence, and in 1720 the bubble burst. The bank collapsed. Thousands were ruined, having exchanged hard cash for now-worthless paper. The memory of this great crash, the most traumatic consequence of the huge debt problem bequeathed by Louis XIV's wars, would haunt the rest of the century. Not until the 1770s were there any further experiments with state banking. Nor was paper money tried again until the 1790s. France fought her 18th century wars without the cheap credit enjoyed by her great cross-Channel rival. Instead, the financial system elaborated under Louis XIV carried on, under increasing strain, until its final breakdown in the 1780s.

What was Louis XIV's cultural legacy?

Louis XIV lived for glory; the men who served him knew that their most important task was to help him achieve it. Later in life the king learnt to accept defeats and misfortunes with dignity and firm resignation, as God's punishment for his sins, but when he was young he treated setbacks more like insults or impertinence. The king of France expected everybody, including other monarchs, to accept his pre-eminence, and also that he should appear effortlessly successful in all he undertook.

Achievements, however small, were fulsomely celebrated in proclamations, sermons, *Te Deums*, medals, and inscriptions. Military victories merited larger triumphal monuments like the arches of 1672 and 1678 at the northern gates of Paris, or the great circular Place des Victoires of 1686 with its colossal statue of the king trampling conquered opponents. Provincial capitals were encouraged during the same proud decade to erect their own royal statues, but even ten years later, when easy victories were a thing of the past, a further grand equestrian effigy was placed at the centre of the newly laid-out Place Louis le Grand (now Vendôme) in the fashionable west end of Paris. These statues stood as reminders of Louis XIV's greatness throughout the 18th century, but were torn down at the fall of the monarchy in 1792.

Most of the larger buildings erected by royal command, however, can still be seen. There is the great colonnade on the eastern façade of the Louvre, incised with the king's monogram. Across the river rises the gilded dome of the Invalides, the vast hospital for military veterans founded in 1674, but not completed until 1706, its portal adorned with another royal statue. Further south stands the Observatory established to promote the work of the Academy of Sciences, not to mention the church and monastery of the Val de Grâce, commemorating the king's seemingly miraculous birth.

In distant Languedoc the most enduring monument of the reign is the Canal du Midi, linking the Atlantic with the Mediterranean; but outside Paris the most striking relic of Louis XIV's time is the Palace of Versailles. It was the grandest royal palace ever built. Surrounded by sprawling gardens, and fountains spraying water brought from miles away by elaborate machinery, it housed the entire court: up to 3,000 people and perhaps twice as many servants. Apart from the brief interval of the regency, it remained the centre of government until 1789, envied and imitated by rulers throughout Europe.

Before the 1680s were over Leopold I and William III (in both his realms) had begun to construct great out-of-town palaces to house their own courts. Over subsequent decades similar seats were established in Spain, Naples, Piedmont, Russia, Sweden and much of small-state Germany. Only in the age of revolution after 1789 did such ostentatious establishments fall out of favour. By then even Napoleon, a great admirer of Louis XIV, thought reoccupation of abandoned Versailles a step too far. Louis XIV found his last royal imitator, however, as late as 1878-9, when the mad king Ludwig (Louis) of Bavaria built and filled two lavish residences in the style of what was remembered as the great age: the *grand siècle*.

Louis XIV's greatest legacy to the 18th century was perhaps the international triumph of the French language. His intention was always to flaunt French power as much through cultural hegemony as military muscle. His policy of founding and funding literary and learned academies was meant to advertise the superiority of the French intellectual world and the royal respect which it enjoyed. Colbert, who enthusiastically supported these initiatives, saw them as complementary to his encouragement of high-quality manufactured goods for export. Before Louis XIV died French had replaced Latin as the language of diplomacy, and was becoming the second language of polite society throughout the continent. At princely courts, indeed, it was sometimes the first.

For francophone elites, Paris was acknowledged as the intellectual capital of Europe, and whatever was written in French reached an immediate international audience. The effect was not always favourable to French official interests: the hostile propaganda of exiled Huguenots, though mostly published in the Dutch Republic, was also in their native language. By the middle of the next century, however, the whole cultural world of the Enlightenment was overwhelmingly francophone. As Voltaire wrote in 1740, "the French language . . . has become almost the universal language. To whom do we owe that?"

Voltaire wrote this in defence of his own forthcoming *Siècle de Louis XIV* (1751), undoubtedly the most important book ever written on the great king. When Louis XIV died, the reputation which he had worked so assiduously to build up was in ruins. He was widely seen as a warmonger

François-Marie Arouet, known as Voltaire

who had inflicted decades of misery on Europe, an extortioner who had impoverished his people, and a cruel bigot who had persecuted harmless religious dissidents. The regency seemed like one great sigh of relief that he was gone. Yet Voltaire, who had grown up while the king was still alive, never shared these attitudes. To him, the age of Louis XIV was one of the great ages of the world, comparable only, if not superior to, ancient Athens, Augustan Rome, and Renaissance Italy.

It was not the wars and conquests of the reign

which impressed Voltaire, although he spent most of his text chronicling them. What he admired above all was the "perfection" of the king's cultural policies, the writers, painters, architects and musicians he patronised and encouraged. Together they had given a style and a polish to French civilisation which was the envy and imitation of Europe. Nor could these achievements have been brought about without the King and the way he ruled. They depended on a strong state, in which "sovereign authority was shored up without contradiction". Louis XIV achieved this after 1661, following the chaos of his minority, and all his faults (which Voltaire admitted, without dwelling on them) were easily excused when compared with the benefits of his style of government.

The great advocate of religious toleration could not avoid condemning the persecution of the Huguenots; but even this, he rather tortuously argued, had its benefits in exporting French skills to less sophisticated countries. "Time," he concluded, "has sealed [Louis XIV's] reputation; and despite everything written against him, his name will never be mentioned without respect." And France, "despite its shocks and losses, is still one of the most flourishing countries on earth, because all the good done by Louis XIV remains, and the bad, which it was difficult not to do in stormy times, has been repaired".

Louis XV and his ministers were wary of Voltaire's praises. They suspected that he was drawing unfavourable contrasts with their own rule. But in fact, in demonstrating what an absolute monarch could achieve, he was offering a spirited defence of the system by which they still governed. When, in the closing years of his reign, Louis XV and his chancellor remodelled and silenced the parlements, Voltaire was loud in his support for such a firm deployment of royal authority. But he found himself isolated among his fellow *philosophes*, and at variance with public opinion.

Far from vindicating the virtues of absolute monarchy, Louis XV's silencing of the parlements underscored the evils of unchecked royal authority. The reforms were abandoned by Louis XVI, whose reign would be marked by repeated attempts to update the monarchy bequeathed by his mighty ancestor, and, ultimately, by its complete overthrow.

What was the final result of the Sun King's ambition?

Louis XIV never acknowledged defeat, although he came close to doing so in 1709. By the time he died he had more subjects and ruled over more extensive territories than he had done when he first came to the throne as a child, or when he assumed personal power in 1661. Whole new provinces, such as Artois, Alsace and Franche Comté had been added to his realms, together with innumerable smaller enclaves and strategic cities like Strasbourg.

Among his targets only Lorraine, despite repeated wartime occupations, had eluded him. Almost by chance his successor was able to achieve that long-cherished ambition. Louis XV married the daughter of Stanislas Leszczynski, the deposed king of Poland. Louis XV failed to restore his father-in-law to the Polish throne, but the upshot of the War of Polish Succession (1733-6) was to install him as Duke of Lorraine. When he died in 1766 the duchy finally passed to France.

French territorial ambitions, therefore, did not die with Louis XIV. Two years after the final acquisition of Lorraine, in fact, without a shot being fired, France also acquired the island of Corsica, which he had chosen not to annex from Genoa in the 1680s, when rebels offered it to him. But in the immediate aftermath of his death, all sides in the great wars between 1688 and 1714 were left exhausted and desperate to avoid further conflicts. For the best part of a generation the French and the British were actually allies. Yet the seeds of further antagonism had already been sown during the great reign: thanks largely to the initiatives of Colbert, Louis XIV had become the ruler of an expanding overseas empire. In North America there were French settlers in Canada, Louisiana (named after the king) and a number of coastal outposts. In the Caribbean were the slave-worked sugar plantations of Martinique, Guadeloupe, and Saint-Domingue, the western half of

Hispaniola. There were also two tropical islands in the Indian Ocean, and a foothold on the Indian subcontinent at Pondicherry.

All these establishments were intended to give France guaranteed supplies of colonial goods, carried exclusively in French ships. And although all the wars of Louis XIV had failed to subdue the Dutch Republic, they certainly broke its virtual stranglehold on Europe's trade with the rest of the world. France, however, was not the only gainer from Dutch decline. By 1713 much of the North American seaboard was settled as British territory, so were major islands in the Caribbean. The East India Company was well established in India. At the Peace of Utrecht Louis XIV only won British recognition of his European gains by ceding to them further American territories and commercial concessions. It was already clear that France and Britain were set to continue as bitter colonial competitors.

By 1740 the exhausted antagonists of 1713-15 had recovered. All Louis XIV's hopes of a Bourbon axis with the Spain of his grandson Philip V were realised by the "Family Compact" of 1733, which was regularly renewed until 1790. And Frederick of Prussia's seizure of Silesia from the Austrians in 1740 offered France the chance to reassert a supremacy over Europe that had been established as "natural" by the great king. In the War of Austrian Succession it was therefore a natural Bourbon reflex to support Prussia in weakening the Habsburgs. An equally natural British reflex was to revive the old alliance with Vienna; and soon a general war was being fought between the same broad alignments as in the last wars of Louis XIV.

This time French armies achieved the victories to which they felt as entitled as under their late king. But the war with the British was now increasingly fought overseas, and although hostilities in Europe ended in 1748, skirmishing in North America and India never really stopped. France therefore, far more extensively than under Louis XIV, found herself simultaneously at war in Europe and across the wider world. By the time peace was made, the financial strain was beginning to tell, and a fresh direct tax, the *vingtième*, had to be introduced – for the first time after, rather than during, a war.

Apparent French triumph at the peace of 1748, in fact, turned out to be the beginning of half a century of trauma. Sated with European gains, Louis XV was now seduced by wily Austrian diplomacy into an alliance with the old Habsburg enemy. It lasted until 1792. But the Austrian purpose in crafting this diplomatic revolution was to wreak revenge if not destruction on Frederick the Great. The result, from 1756, was to suck Louis XV into a war on Prussia for no obvious advantage, while the British, betrayed by the Austrians, allied with Frederick. And when the French army confronted the Prussians at Rossbach in 1756, it was routed.

The result of this Seven Years' War overseas was even worse. Three years after the Battle of Rossbach in 1759 the bulk of the French navy was destroyed by the British in two great sea battles, while a relentless blockade blighted overseas trade. Cut off from her colonies, France lost Canada, Guadeloupe and most of her footholds in India. At the peace signed in 1763 Guadeloupe was regained, and colonial trade rapidly recovered, but French prestige had been shattered, the war had cost twice as much as its predecessor, and the burden of state debt was higher in real terms than when Louis XIV died.

The debt was never cleared. Instead, massive new sums were spent on rebuilding the navy and reforming the army for a war of revenge against Britain – "the modern Carthage". When, in the 1770s, the 13 colonies of British North America renounced their allegiance to George III, the opportunity appeared to have come. If Britain could be deprived of her American dominions, her empire would be destroyed and France could dominate Europe's colonial trade.

Spurred by these ambitions, Louis XVI offered military assistance to the rebels. While the Austrian alliance kept Europe quiet, France was able for the first time in the century to devote all her resources to the colonial conflict, capturing control of the Atlantic long enough to ship an army across it. With the help of this army, the British were defeated, and the United States secured its independence. It was the last great triumph of the Bourbon monarchy's armed forces.

But the victory was hollow. Independent America did not switch its commercial allegiance to France, and the persistent incursions of its merchants forced the opening of the French Caribbean colonies to all flags. In contrast, worldwide British trade, far from being destroyed, flourished as never before. And meanwhile the debts of the French monarchy finally spiralled out of control. Louis XVI and his ministers recognised that they were unsustainable without reforms that must change forever the absolute monarchy created by Louis XIV. Yet resistance to reform by the very elites and institutions through which he had ruled simply brought on bankruptcy, and the terminal crisis which developed into the French Revolution.

The strain of living up to the standards and ambitions set by Louis XIV had proved too much. The world had changed in the three generations since his death, but the domestic system which had served him so well had not. France still had the resources to dominate the European continent, as the next generation was to show; but it took a revolution to unlock them.

Napoleon, in fact, came far closer to the universal monarchy so often feared to be Louis XIV's aim than the Sun King ever did. Like most of the revolutionaries, Napoleon blamed the failures and disappointments of the old monarchy since the 1750s on an "unnatural" Austrian alliance which

Louis XIV would never have made. Although Emperor Napoleon, like Louis XIV, eventually married a Habsburg princess, most of his continental campaigns were waged against her father, the traditional enemy.

At these moments, the Austrians instinctively – naturally – turned to their old British allies. And in the face of British sea power, Napoleon was never able to restore the old French colonial empire. While he dominated the continent, the British finally won the contest for colonial dominance. With their Austrian allies, they were eventually even able to force the ruler of France to surrender completely, and to give up territory he had conquered. It was true that the British could not have done it without Russia, an empire which Louis XIV had scarcely deigned to recognise. Nevertheless, the downfall of Napoleon marked the final defeat of the ambitions and pretensions which had dazzled and driven French policy ever since the time of the Sun King.

A SHORT CHRONOLOGY

1638 Birth of Louis 'the God-Given', 5 September

1642 Death of Richelieu

1643 Death of Louis XIII; accession of Louis XIV; Regency of Anne of Austria

1648 Peace of Westphalia; outbreak of the Fronde

1651 Majority of Louis XIV; end of Regency

1652 End of the Fronde

1654 Coronation of Louis XIV

1659 Peace of the Pyrenees

1660 Marriage of Louis XIV to Infanta Maria Teresa of Spain

1661 Death of Mazarin; Louis XIV takes personal control; fall of Fouquet

1665 Death of Philip IV of Spain

1666 Death of Anne of Austria

1667-8 War of Devolution

1669 Peace of the Church

1672-8 Dutch War, concluded by Peace of Nijmegen

1673 Parlement's right of remonstrance restricted

1675 Revolts in Bordeaux and Brittany

1679-84 Reunions

1681 Annexation of Strasbourg

1682 Four Gallican Articles restricting papal authority; bombardment of Genoa; court established at Versailles

1683 Death of the Queen and Colbert; Turks unsuccessfully besiege Vienna

1684 Truce of Ratisbon: Louis XIV marries Mme de Maintenon

1685 Revocation of Edict of Nantes

1688-97 Nine Years' War

1688 Invasion of Palatinate; 'Glorious Revolution' brings William III to British thrones

1691 Death of Louvois

1693-4 Disastrous weather, plague and famine

1695 Capitation introduced

1697 Peace of Ryswick

1698 First Partition Treaty

1700 Second Partition Treaty; death of Carlos II of Spain; Anjou becomes Spanish king

1702-14 War of the Spanish Succession

1702-9 Camisard Rebellion in Languedoc

1708-9 Great Winter

1709 Destruction of Port Royal

1711 Death of the Grand Dauphin; death of Emperor Joseph

1712 Death of Duke de Bourgogne

1713 *Unigenitus*; peace of Utrecht

1714 Legitimised princes placed in succession; peace of Rastatt

1715 Death of Louis XIV, 1 September

BIBLIOGRAPHY

Eyewitnesses
A number of famous observers have moulded historical perceptions of Louis XIV and his reign.

Cardinal de Retz (1613-1679), one of the leaders of the Parisian Fronde, composed his *Memoirs* between 1675 and 1677, a vivid account of the upheavals of the first reign that was published after the king's death in 1717. They seek, like most memoirs, to vindicate the role of their author, but are full of colourful accounts of major incidents in which he was involved.

Mme de Sévigné (1626-1696) was a prolific letter-writer, perhaps the best-known in French literary history. 1372 of her letters from between 1648 and her death have survived. More than half were to her daughter, recounting gossip and observation both from the life of the court and capital and her husband's estates in Brittany. Wife of a marquis, she was well connected in noble and literary society, and admired for her style in her own lifetime, although the first printed collection of her letters did not appear until 1725.

Ezechiel Spanheim (1629-1710), a German diplomat sent in 1680 as envoy extraordinary to France. He remained there until 1689. On returning to Berlin he wrote *Relation de la Cour de France en 1690*, a report on his mission. It was a long and detailed account of how France was governed. Parts of his report were first published in 1781, and a full text only in 1900.

Marquis de Dangeau (1638-1720), a soldier, courtier and friend of the king, he kept a detailed day-to-day diary of life at the court of Versailles from 1684 until his death. Its existence was well known to contemporaries, including Saint-Simon (below) who deplored what he saw as its colourless sycophancy in chronicling the details of royal service. The *Journal* was not published until 1854, in nineteen volumes.

Pierre Jurieu (1637-1713), a Protestant pastor who left France in 1681 as persecution of the Huguenots increased. From exile in the Dutch Republic he denounced the iniquities of Catholic persecutions and doctrine in a bitter stream of pamphlets. It is generally (though not universally) accepted that he was the anonymous author of *Les Soupirs de la France esclave qui aspire à la liberté* (*The Groans of France enslav'd, aspiring to Freedom*, 1689), a pamphlet series which is the fiercest indictment of Louis XIV's tyranny.

Elisabeth Charlotte d'Orléans ('Liselotte') (1672-1722), daughter of the Elector Palatine, second wife of Louis XIV's brother, Monsieur, and mother of the Regent Philippe d'Orléans. A forthright German, she wrote regularly to her relatives with pitiless and sardonic observations about court life in Louis XIV's later years. The first selection of these lively private letters, mostly written in German, appeared in 1857.

Duke de Saint-Simon (1675-1755), the most celebrated chronicler of the court of Versailles in his *Memoirs*, mostly written between 1739 and 1750. They run from 1691 to 1723. A prickly man, obsessed by his status, he deplored the way Louis XIV governed through "vile bourgeois" and dreamed of a restoration of aristocratic power. His was a life of constant disappointment, reflected in waspish disparagement of almost everyone. Confiscated by the government on his death as too critical of people still alive or remembered, extracts from the memoirs began to appear in 1781, and the full text only became available over the next century.

François de Salignac de la Mothe Fénelon (1651-1715), tutor to the Duke de Bourgogne and Archbishop of Cambrai. He was the leading light in a circle that placed hopes of reform in the eventual rule of his pupil. His *Aventures de Télémaque* (1699), published without his consent, were a manual of kingship implicitly critical of Louis XIV. He never published even more directly critical writings, such as the (never-sent) *Letter to Louis XIV* (1695). He spent the last sixteen years of his life exiled in his diocese after involvement with suspect religious doctrines. His writings were widely read over the next century.

Baron de Montesquieu (1689-1755), a magistrate from Bordeaux whose best known work, *De l'Esprit des Lois* (1748) was one of the most influential books of social and political theory of the 18th century. But he grew up under Louis XIV, and made his name in 1721 with the thinly anonymous *Persian Letters*, which satirised French institutions and society as left by the great king.

Secondary reading
(All these books are in English, but many of the most important works on the subject are in French. Readers of French can track them in the bibliographies of the works listed below)

Beik, William, *Absolutism and Society in seventeenth century France: State Power and Provincial Aristocracy in Languedoc,* Cambridge University Press, 1985.

Beik, William, 'The Absolutism of Louis XIV as social collaboration' *Past and Present*, 188 (2005), 199-224.

Bergin, Joseph, *Church, Society and Religious Change in France, 1680-1730*, Yale University Press, 2009

Bergin, Joseph, *The Politics of Religion in Early Modern France*, Yale University Press, 2014

Bluche, François, *Louis XIV*, Blackwell, 1990

Bonney, Richard, *Political Change in France under Richelieu and Mazarin, 1624-1661*, Oxford University Press, 1978

Bonney, Richard, *The King's Debts. Finance and Politics in France, 1589-1661*, Oxford University Press, 1981

Burke, Peter, *The Fabrication of Louis XIV*, Yale University Press, 1992

Cole, Charles Woolsey, *Colbert and a Century of French Mercantilism*, 2 vols., Columbia University Press, 1939

Collins, James B., *The State in Early Modern France*,

Cambridge University Press, 2009

Goubert, Pierre, *Louis XIV and Twenty Million Frenchmen*, Vintage, 1972

Hamscher, Albert N., *The Parlement of Paris after the Fronde, 1653-1673*, University of Pittsburgh Press, 1976

Hatton, Ragnhild, *Louis XIV and his World*, Thames and Hudson, 1972.

Henshall, Nicholas, *The Myth of Absolutism: Change and Continuity in Early Modern European Monarchy*, Longman, 1992

Hurt, John, J. *Louis XIV and the Parlements. The Assertion of Royal Authority*, Manchester University Press, 2002

Lynn, John A., *Giant of the Grand Siècle. The French Army, 1610-1715*, Cambridge University Press, 1997

Lynn, John A., *The Wars of Louis XIV, 1667-1714*, Longman, 1999

Mettam, Roger, *Power and Faction in Louis XIV's France*, Blackwell, 1988

Monahan, W. Gregory, *Let God Arise. The War and Rebellion of the Camisards*, Oxford University Press, 2014

Potter, Mark, *Corps and Clienteles. Public Finance and Political Change in France, 1688 - 1715*, Ashgate, 2003

Ranum, Orest, *The Fronde. A French Revolution*, Norton,

1993

Rowlands, Guy, *The Dynastic State and the Army under Louis XIV*, Cambridge University Press, 2002

Rowlands, Guy, *The Financial Decline of a Great Power. War, Influence, and Money in Louis XIV's France*, Oxford University Press, 2012

Rowlands, Guy, *Dangerous and Dishonest Men. The International Bankers of Louis XIV's France*, Palgrave, 2014.

Scoville, Warren C., *The Persecution of the Huguenots and French Economic Development, 1680-1720*, University of California Press, 1960

Sonnino, Paul (ed. and trans.) *Memoirs for the Instruction of the Dauphin by Louis XIV*, New York, 1970

Sonnino, Paul, *Louis XIV and the Origins of the Dutch War*, Cambridge University Press, 1988

Sturdy, David J., *Richelieu and Mazarin. A Study in Statesmanship*, Palgrave, 2004

Sturdy, David J., *Louis XIV*, Palgrave, 1998

Wolf, John B., *Louis XIV*, Norton, 1968

ⒼⒼ CONNELL GUIDES

MORE IN OUR NEW HISTORY SERIES

Guides
The French Revolution
Winston Churchill
World War One
The Third Reich
Stalin
Lenin
Nelson
Napoleon
The Cold War
The American Civil War
The Normans

Russia and its Rulers
The Amerian Civil Rights Movement

Short Guides
Britain after World War Two
Edward VI
Mary I
The General Strike
The Suffragettes
President Truman
President Lincoln

"Connell Guides should be required reading in every school in the country.
Julian Fellowes, creator of Downton Abbey

"What Connell Guides do is bring immediacy and clarity: brevity with depth. They unlock the complex and offer students an entry route."
Colin Hall, Head of Holland Park School

"These guides are a godsend. I'm so glad I found them."
Jessica Enthoven, A Level student, St Mary's Calne

"Completely brilliant. I wish I were young again with these by my side. It's like being in a room with marvellous tutors. You can't really afford to be without them, and they are a joy to read."
Joanna Lumley

To buy any of these guides, or for more information, go to
www.connellguides.com
Or contact us on (020)79932644 / info@connellguides.com

LITERATURE GUIDES

Novels and poetry
Emma
Far From the Madding Crowd
Frankenstein
Great Expectations
Hard Times
Heart of Darkness
Jane Eyre
Lord of the Flies
Mansfield Park
Middlemarch
Mrs Dalloway
Paradise Lost
Persuasion
Pride and Prejudice
Tess of the D'Urbervilles
The Canterbury Tales
The Great Gatsby
The Poetry of Robert Browning
The Waste Land
To Kill A Mockingbird
Wuthering Heights

Shakespeare
A Midsummer Night's Dream
Antony and Cleopatra
Hamlet
Julius Caesar
King Lear
Macbeth
Othello
Romeo and Juliet
The Second Tetralogy
The Tempest
Twelfth Night

Modern texts
A Doll's House
A Room with a View
A Streetcar Named Desire
An Inspector Calls
Animal Farm
Atonement
Beloved
Birdsong
Hullabaloo
Never Let Me Go
Of Mice and Men
Rebecca
Spies
The Bloody Chamber
The Catcher in the Rye
The History Boys
The Road
Vernon God Little
Waiting for Godot

NEW
A Short History of English Literature
American literature
Dystopian literature
How to read a poem
How to read Shakespeare
The Gothic
The poetry of Christina Rossetti
Women in literature

INDEX

A
Absolutism 29–32, 40–41, 59, 101
American colonies 102–106
American Independence 105–106
Anne of Austria (mother) 4–6, 7, 15–19, 24, 27, 49, 62
Austrian Habsburgs 6, 8, 13, 16, 64, 78, 83, 103–107
Authoritarianism *see* Absolutism

B
Beik, William H. 32
Bernini, Gian Lorenzo 47–48
Blenheim, battle of 80
Bonaparte, Napoleon 5, 65, 97, 106–107
Bonney, Richard 31
Broussel, Pierre 15–16
Burke, Peter 57

C
Camisard rebellion 65–66
Capitation (poll-tax) 76, 80
Carlos II of Spain 51–52, 55, 77–78
Catholicism 48–49, 56, 64
Chamillart, Michel 81
Charles I of England 21, 27
Charles II of England 52–53
Charles VI, Holy Roman Emperor (*earlier* Archduke) 78–79
Clement XI, Pope 66–67
Colbert, Jean-Baptiste 26, 33–36, 42–48, 57, 59, 62, 72, 98
Colbert, Seigneley 62, 72–73
College of Four Nations (*Institut de France*) 23–24, 25
Concordat of Bologna (1516) 65
Corsica 102
Cromwell, Oliver 27

D
Desmaretz, Nicolas 81
Dessert, Daniel 57
Duels 39

Dutch War 67, 72

E
Edict of Fontainebleau (1685) 56
Edict of Nantes (1598) 48–49, 56, 64, 87
England 16, 27, 83–84, 102–107
Enlightenment 98
Eugene, Prince of Savoy 80, 84
"Extraordinary" expedients 9, 22, 41, 76

F
"Family Compact" (1733) 103
Fénelon, François 90
Fleury, André-Hercule de 92
Fontainebleau, royal residence 49–50
Fouquet, Nicolas 25–26, 33–34
France
    bureaucracy 85–86
    church and monasteries 47, 66–67
    cultural golden age 46–47, 95–101
    duels in 39
    economic crises 80–81, 84–87, 94–95, 105–106
    economic stimulus 45–46
    famine and disease 20–21, 40–41, 68, 75, 82, 87
    manufacturing 46–47, 98
    military expenses 75–76
    during minority of Louis XIV 5–8
    navy 46, 72, 75, 105
    peace negotiations 43, 51–53, 55–56, 82–84
    state crises 14–15
    territorial expansion 8–9, 50–57, 69–74, 84, 101–103, 105
    weather 67–68, 80
Franche Comté (region) 53–54, 76
Francis I of France 49
Frederick the Great 103–104
French language 97–98
French Revolution 5, 106
Frondes (rebellions)

cause and end of 15–19, 32
defeat of rebels 19–21
duels 39
"Fronde of the Magistrates"
    (first) 11, 15–21, 32
"Fronde of the Princes" (second)
    19–21
Huguenots during 48–49
and Jansenists 47
and reform 87–88
venality and 11, 42–43

G
Gallicanism 65
Gaston, Duke of Orléans (brother)
    6, 19–20
Germany 8, 16, 18, 22, 53, 64, 70–71,
    73, 97
Grands, Les (nobility at court) 37
"Great Winter" (1709) 68, 80

H
Habsburgs *see* Austrian Habsburgs
Hamscher, Albert 58
Hatton, Ragnhild 59
Henri, Prince de Condé (cousin) 6,
    15–20, 27, 51
Henry IV of France (grandfather)
    48, 49
Henshall, Nicholas 59
Holy Roman Empire 55, 63–64; *see
    also* Leopold I, Holy Roman
    Emperor
Huguenots 48, 56, 64, 87, 100
Hurt, John J. 58

I
Innocent XII, Pope 56, 64–66
Intendants 10–12, 24

J
James II of England 49, 64, 70,
    73–74, 79
Jansenism 47–48, 66–67, 90–91
Jesuits 47, 91
Joseph I, Holy Roman Emperor 83

K
"King's Mouth" food department 61

L
Languedoc, Canal du Midi 96–97
Law, John 94
Le Tellier, Michel 26, 36, 62
League of Augsburg 64, 69
Lens, battle of 15
Leopold I, Holy Roman Emperor
    52–56, 63–64, 69, 74, 77–78,
    97
Lille, battle of 80
Lionne, Hugues de 26
Lits de justice (sovereign rulings)
    12–15, 20, 42, 93
Lorraine (region) 54, 74, 84, 102
Louis, Duke of Bourgogne 68–69,
    89–90
Louis, Grand Dauphin (son) 42–43,
    50, 61, 68
Louis, Prince de Condé (Duke of
    Enghien) 6
Louis Alexandre, Count of Toulouse
    (son) 69, 89, 92
Louis Auguste, Duke of Maine (son)
    69, 89, 92
Louis XIII of France (father) 4–8
Louis XIV of France 4–5
    absolutism 29–36, 40–49, 59, 101
    advisors to 9, 29, 36–40
    appetite 61, 63
    bathing 60
    chronology 108–110
    coronation 22
    cultural legacy 95–101
    cultural patronage 46–47
    death 61, 84, 89
    early majority 19, 22–25
    failings 62–69
    fashion of 60
    during the Frondes 16, 19–20, 49
    height 61
    historical views on 29–32, 57–59,
        85–88, 98–101
    illnesses 23, 63
    marriages 27–28, 50–51, 61–62

memoirs 42–43
minority 5–8, 14–15, 21
mistresses 50–51, 56, 61–62, 63
portraits 35, 61, 71
preparations for power 22–29
in public 19
religion and the church 47, 56, 90
residences 48–50
rivals 26
statues 96
succession issues 68–69, 77, 88–89, 92
ten facts about 60–61
titles and mottoes 4, 30–31
wigs 60
work ethic 38–40, 63
Louis XV of France (grandson) 92–93, 101–102, 104
Louis XVI of France (great-grandson) 93, 101, 105–107
Louisiana (U.S.A.) 60
Louvois, François-Michel Le Tellier 52, 55, 57, 62, 71, 75
Louvre, royal residence 48
Ludwig (Louis) of Bavaria 97
Luxembourg 55, 74

M

Maintenon, Françoise de (mistress and wife) 56, 61–62, 63
Malplaquet, battle of 82
Mancini, Marie 24
Maria Theresa of Spain (wife) 24, 27–28, 28, 50–51, 61, 77
Marlborough, John Churchill, 1st Duke 80, 83
Marly, royal residence 50
Mazarin, Jules, Cardinal 5–6, 23
College of Four Nations (*Institut de France*) 23–24, 25
excesses 12–15
exiles 18–20
and the Frondes 17–21
illness and death 28–29
preparations of Louis XIV 22–29
revenue raising 8–12

on state reforms 16
Mazarinades (pamphlets) 14
Mettam, Roger 58
Monahan, Gregory 86–87
Money 81, 86, 95
Montespan, Athénaïs de (mistress) 51, 69
Mousnier, Roland 31

N

Netherlands
French expansion quest 16–17, 20, 43, 51–54, 59, 67, 70–74, 79, 84
trading dominance 46, 53, 94, 103
Nobility 37–38, 44–45, 57–58, 76, 87–88

O

Oudenarde, battle of 80

P

Pagès, Georges 85–86
Palais Royal 49
Pamphleteering 14
Paper money (*billets de monnaie*) 81, 86, 95
Parlements
and *lits de justice* 12–15, 20
protests in 15–17, 20, 87
regency period 93
remonstrances 38, 58
restrictions on 20, 24–25, 30–31, 38, 101
venality in 11–13
Particelli d'Emery 8, 12, 14
Paulette (hereditary tax) 13, 25
Peace of Carlowitz 74
Peace of Rastatt 84
Peace of Ryswick 38, 79
Peace of the Church 47–48, 66
Peace of the Pyrenees 27, 51
Peace of Utrecht 84
Peace of Westphalia 16, 22, 59
Pensions 45
Perrault, Charles 47
Phélypeaux family 36

Philip IV of Spain 6, 11, 24, 27–28
Philip V of Spain (grandson; *earlier* Duke of Anjou) 34, 69, 78, 82–84, 103
Philippe I, Duke of Orléans (brother) 49
Philippe II, Duke of Orléans (Regent) 89–94, *91*
Poland 102
Polysynodie (council-based government) 92–94
Pope Clement XI 66–67
Pope Innocent XII 56, 64–66
Port Royal monastery 47, 66–67
Protestantism 27, 48–49, 56, 62, 64–66, 84, 87, 89
Provence 26
Prussia 103–104

Q

Quietism (cult) 90

R

Raison d'Etat (long-termism) 8
Ramillies, battle of 80
Rebellions *see* Frondes
Recoinages (minting coins) 86
Religion 27, 48–49, 56, 62, 64–66, 84, 87, 89, 100
Retz, Jean François Paul de Gondi de 20, 111
Revisionism 32, 58–59
Rheims Cathedral 22
Richelieu, Cardinal 5–12
Rigaud, Hyacinthe, portrait of Louis XIV *71*
Rossbach, battle of 104–105
Rothkrug, Lionel 87
Rowlands, Guy 58, 86
Royal residences 48–50, 97
Rubens, Peter Paul, portrait of Anne of Austria *7*
Russia 107

S

Saint-Germain, royal residence 48–49
St. Louis Chamber, reform demands 13–16
Scoville, Warren C. 87
Secret Treaty of Dover 52
Seven Years' War 105
Sonnino, Paul 59
Spain, war with 6–8, 15–18, 22, 24–27, 51–55, 59
  Succession War 43, 68, 73–74, 76–80, 86

T

Tax revolts 7–8, 26
Taxation 7–9, 12–13, 21, 24–26, 43–46, 76, 84, 104
Theatres 46–47
Thèse royale (historical thesis) 29, 57–59
Thirty Years' War 11
Traitants (financiers) 9–10, 12–14, 24, 34, 76, 81, 86, 94
Truce of Ratisbon 55–56, 69, 74
Tuileries, royal residence 48
Turenne, Henri de 19, 27, 48–49, 51

U

Unigenitus (papal bull) 67, 90–91

V

Val-de Grâce (church) 4, 96
Vauban, Sébastien Le Prestre de 75, 80
Venality and venal offices 10–11, 42–44, 76, 80, 88, 94
Versailles, Palace of 45, 50, 62, 68, 85, 92–93, 97
Villars, Claude Louis Hector de *83*
Vingtième (tax) 104
Voltaire (François-Marie Arouet) 98–101, *99*

W

War of Austrian Succession 103
War of Devolution 51–52, 72
War of Polish Succession 102
War with Spain *see* Spain, war with
Weather, "little ice age" 67–68, 80
Wigs 60
William III of England 53–54, 70–74, 77–80, 84, 97

Many thanks to Alistair Dougall for years of help and advice over Louis XIV

First published in 2017 by
Connell Guides
Spye Arch House
Spye Park
Lacock
Wiltshire
SN15 2PR

10 9 8 7 6 5 4 3 2 1

Copyright © Connell Guides Publishing Ltd.
All rights reserved. No part of this publication
may be reproduced, stored in a retrieval system or transmitted in any
form, or by any means (electronic, mechanical, or otherwise) without
the prior written permission of both the copyright owners
and the publisher.

A CIP catalogue record for this book is available from the British Library.
ISBN 978-1-911187-69-1

Design © Nathan Burton

Assistant Editors and typeset by:
Brian Scrivener and Paul Woodward

Printed and bound by CPI Group (UK) Ltd, Croydon, CR0 4YY

www.connellguides.com